THE
RED HEIFER
RITUAL

THE RED HEIFER RITUAL

The Last Piece of the Third Temple Puzzle

By Mondo Gonzales

THE RED HEIFER RITUAL

© 2023 by Mondo Gonzales
Blessed Hope Publishing

All rights reserved. No part of this book may be reproduced in any form by any electronic or mechanical means including photocopying, recording, or information storage and retrieval without permission in writing from the author or publisher.

ISBN: 978-1-962356-00-8

Book Website:
prophecywatchers.com/red-heifer

Printed in the United States of America

Cover & Map Design by Daniel M. Wright

Colorized cover illustration derived from
"Sacrifice of a Red Cow by the Israelites"
Artist/Engraver unknown; circa 1700 -1800
Gift of the J.G. de Groot Jamin Bequest, Amsterdam
Public domain – Rijksmuseum.nl

Table of Contents

Chapter 1: Introduction — 1
   Modern Israel's Founding and Religious Climate — 2
   Why Should We Even Care About the Red Heifer? — 3
   Conclusion — 12

Chapter 2: The Red Heifer in the Bible — 13
   The Red Heifer Commandment: Numbers 19:1-22 — 14
   Numbers 19:1-6 — 15
   Numbers 19:7-13 — 18
   Numbers 19:14-22 — 20

Chapter 3: The Red Heifer in Rabbinic Tradition — 25
   How old must the red heifer be in order to be slaughtered? — 29
   How many non-red hairs will disqualify the heifer? — 32
   Where is the location the red heifer is supposed to be slaughtered? — 36
   Is it okay if the heifer is not raised in Israel or can it be purchased from Gentiles (non-Jews)? — 40

Chapter 4: The Rabbis are Changing Their Thinking in Recent Years — 47

Chapter 5: The Pre-Temple Preparations — 57

Chapter 6: The Modern Search for the Red Heifer — 65
   The Beginning Searches (1980s-2020) — 65
   The Latest 5 Red Heifers (Arrived in Israel September 15, 2022) — 67

Chapter 7: What is the New Testament Significance of the Red Heifer — 73

Chapter 8: Your Favorite Prophecy Teachers Respond to the Red Heifer Movement — 81

Chapter 9: Seeking a Balanced Biblical Outlook on the Red Heifer Movement — 107

What Does the New Testament Teach about the Second Temple and Its Destruction?   *107*

What is the Spiritual Condition of National Israel Today?   *115*

My Answers to the Three Questions About the Red Heifer Movement   *121*

Chapter 10: Concluding Thoughts on the Red Heifer Movement   **129**

Appendix 1: Alfred Edersheim and The Temple, Its Ministry and Services as They Were at the Time of Jesus Christ   **131**

Appendix 2: Josephus Discusses the Red Heifer   **136**

Chapter 1: Introduction

We are living in exciting times! Ever since Israel became a nation in 1948, prophecy watchers have been eagerly awaiting the Lord's return to call His bride home. In the midst of the present convergence of dozens of prophetic signs, on September 15, 2022, five red heifers were shipped from Texas and landed in Israel. In this book, you will be able to understand the prophetic significance of this arrival and be given the background to recognize the importance of the red heifer movement.

Although our story begins with Moses around 1400 B.C., it is alive and active in our current time! The first thing to address is, "What is a heifer?" Simply put, a heifer is a 2 or 3-year-old female cow. It is not a calf nor is it a bull (male cow). The excitement about these five heifers in Israel and around the world for many Christians has become quite intense. There is a cautious optimism that at least one of these red heifers will remain qualified and will be ritually slaughtered in 2023. I will explain later why I think 2023 could be the year.

There also is the risk for some Christians to misunderstand exactly what I mean by saying we are living in exciting times. There are dozens, if not hundreds, of prophetic passages that help us to understand the events leading up to the 2nd coming of Jesus. Many of these prophecies contain information that is quite serious and reveal horrible judgments which are going to be coming upon the earth during the 7-year tribulation period. Billions will perish, and Jesus said this time period is unlike anything that has ever occurred in the history of the creation (Mark 13:19). The Bible also reveals that the Jewish people are going to be deceived by the antichrist and will have severe persecution during this period.

Am I excited for the death and judgment, or the building of the Third Temple when seen in isolation? Not at all! When prophecy watchers get excited, it is because the signs we see being fulfilled all point to the imminent return of Jesus when He makes all things right. We are excited about that, and it does not mean that we condone or approve of the new world order or the cashless system that is arriving, or even specifically endorsing the slaughter of the red heifer. This book is intended to help the average Christian understand the prophetic significance of the red heifer movement and also the preparations that have been made to build the Third Temple.

In order to accomplish this understanding, it would be helpful to briefly outline the prophetic importance and timeline of how Israel became a nation in 1948, and also how the Temple Mount continues to be a place of tension between the Jewish people and its neighbors.

Modern Israel's Founding and Religious Climate

David Ben Gurion, the first prime minister of Israel, declared to the world the independent state of Israel on May 14, 1948. The situation in 1948 was tense, as Israel was immediately attacked by its Arab neighbors the following day (May 15, 1948), but after a drawn-out series of conflicts, Israel signed armistice agreements with all the attackers by July 1949. Israel was an official country and became a member of the world of the United Nations on May 11, 1949.

There were several other skirmishes in the next decade, but the next one having prophetic implications was the Six-Day War from June 5-10, 1967. For the first time since AD 70, the Jewish people had control of Jerusalem!

Many people might not know that Israel was founded by those who would generally consider themselves socialist. Even though it was founded as a parliamentary democracy, it was not overly influenced by the religious demographic. In order to understand the current prophetic atmosphere in Israel and about the Temple Mount, one must recognize how different the country is now from its founding 75 years ago. The typical Jewish religious rabbinic opinion in the mid-20th century was that modern Israel was founded by secularists, and therefore had no real religious legitimacy in their eyes. They held the belief that God Himself would miraculously create a Jewish state if that was His will.

So, let's venture back to 1967 when Israel conquered its enemies once again and regained control of Jerusalem - and more specifically, the Temple Mount area. The Jewish people had been forbidden to pray at the Western Wall and on the Temple Mount after the 1949 armistice agreements and had no access to western Jerusalem. After the end of the 1967 war, over 200,000 Jews flocked to the Western Wall to pray. This was seen as the largest Jewish pilgrimage to the Western Wall since AD 70.

However, this nationalistic fervor would not last, as Defense Minister, Moshe Dayan, a self-proclaimed atheist, made an agreement on June 17, 1967, with the Muslim religious authority over the Temple Mount known as the Waqf. Jews would be allowed to visit inside the Temple Mount (but could not pray) and have access to the Western Wall, but full religious authority would remain with the Islamic Waqf over the Temple Mount. Political and security sovereignty would remain with the State of Israel. There were a variety of diverse religious opinions at the time related to this decision. It would be helpful to note that the chief rabbis had issued a declaration that it was forbidden for any Jew to enter inside the Temple Mount area. For them, this political decision by Moshe Dayan was actually helpful to enforce their declaration forbidding all Jews (especially religious) from going up on the Temple Mount. There have always been a few orthodox religious groups who ignored these prohibitions, but the consensus of Rabbis has always been to forbid Jews to go up on the Temple Mount.

The status quo of the Temple Mount has ebbed and flowed very little since 1967. However, during the last 15 years (and especially since November 1, 2022, with the latest election of Benjamin Netanyahu and the most religious government in the history of modern Israel), there have been tremendous ramifications for the status quo of the Temple Mount, the coming Third Temple, and of course the red heifer.

Why Should We Even Care About the Red Heifer?

When it comes to understanding eschatology (the study of last things), there is a wide diversity of beliefs among genuine Christians today. It is not my goal here to survey all the various beliefs, but there are some believers who see no significance to Israel becoming a nation nor of them gaining control over Jerusalem. Others view it as interesting and that it probably means something, but they do not make it an important enough topic to address in a Sunday morning sermon. On the other hand, I have known other believers who only read eschatological texts and don't have a good grasp on other areas of theology. As always, we should maintain a proper balance. The most important topic to be competent in as a follower of Jesus is to be able to share and articulate the good news that Jesus is the only way for people to be reconciled to God the Father (Acts 4:12; John 14:6; Romans 3:23; 6:23; 5:8; 10:9).

  At the same time, Jesus gave us instructions to be watching and ready for His return at any moment. Jesus scolded the Pharisees of His day for not understanding Messianic prophecy related to His first coming, *"And the Pharisees and Sadducees came, and to test Him they asked Him to show them a sign from heaven. He answered them, "When it is evening, you say, 'It will be fair weather, for the sky is red.' And in the morning, 'It will be stormy today, for the sky is red and threatening.' You know how to interpret the appearance of the sky, but you cannot interpret the signs of the times. An evil and adulterous generation seeks for a sign, but no sign will be given to it except the sign of Jonah." So, He left them and departed"* (Matthew 16:1-4).

  When it comes to Messianic prophecy related to His second coming, Jesus gave extensive descriptions of what the end of the age would be like in various sermons (Luke 17:22-37) and in what is known as the Olivet Discourse (Matthew 24-25; Mark 13; Luke 21). After giving precise details, He commanded all of His followers, *"Therefore stay awake—for you do not know when the master of the house will come, in the evening, or at midnight, or when the rooster crows, or in the morning— lest he come suddenly and find you asleep. And what I say to you <u>I say to all:</u> **<u>Be Watching</u>**!"* (Mark 13:35-37). As a follower of Jesus, we do not have the luxury of dismissing Jesus' words or else we fall into the same category as the 1st century Pharisees. We are not required to become experts in eschatology, but we are required to have some sort of understanding so that we know what to watch for as Jesus said we should.

One of those prophetic markers to watch for is the preparations to build, or the actual building, of the Third Temple in Jerusalem on the Temple Mount. I will cover those preparations in a subsequent chapter, but for now, it would be helpful to share why we believe a Third Temple will be built and how it connects to the red heifer.

The Bible does not always give us the absolute complete picture or details of how prophecy is to be fulfilled. For example, consider the prophecy that the Messiah would be born in Bethlehem of Judea, *"But you, O Bethlehem Ephrathah, who are too little to be among the clans of Judah, from you shall come forth for me one who is to be ruler in Israel, whose coming forth is from of old, from ancient days"* (Micah 5:2). All it reveals is the location of where the Messiah would come from. It does not reveal the how or the when. As we come to the gospels, we learn how God moved a pagan Roman emperor (Proverbs 21:1) to issue a census to get Joseph and Mary to travel to their ancestral home from Nazareth (80 miles away) in order to be registered. It was at this time that Jesus was born in Bethlehem, as we learn in Matthew 2. Thus, Micah 5:2 was fulfilled in an unexpected way.

Prophecy is most often a "snapshot" of the circumstances in a particular time and place. The prophet is given a word or a dream or a vision of this time period. When it comes to understanding why prophecy watchers expect a Third Temple, we see a snapshot into the future by several different prophets. Each one of them gives us an insight concerning the final "day of the Lord" which is also called the "tribulation period" or the "70th week of Daniel."

Let's begin in the Old Testament with the prophet Daniel. We do not have space to cover the entire 70 weeks of Daniel, but what concerns us is the last verse of chapter 9, which describes the events of the last week that are yet to be fulfilled. Daniel writes, *"And he shall make a strong covenant with many for one week, and for half of the week he shall <u>put an end to sacrifice and offering</u>. And on the wing of* *abominations shall come one who makes desolate, until the decreed end is poured out on the desolator"* (Daniel 9:27).

From this passage, we learn that at the "half" point of the week (the 3.5-year mark out of the 7 years), the antichrist will put an end to sacrifices and offerings. Which sacrifices? Which offerings? The Temple was destroyed in AD 70, and there have not been sacrifices in Jerusalem on the Temple Mount for over 1900 years. Let's go back to the concept that Daniel is getting a snapshot of a future time period. What he sees in this future end-time scenario are sacrifices and offerings taking place. This can seem very confusing because there is no temple today for those sacrifices and offerings to take place. So, what should we conclude? We could say that Daniel was possibly speaking figuratively or symbolically (some people take this position). It does not make much sense, because as soon as you begin to spiritualize interpretations, there is no solid conclusion. It is almost completely subjective to the reader. Secondly, we could say that it was already fulfilled as other Bible teachers claim. This does not make much sense either because the purposes of the 70-week prophecy as found in Daniel 9:24-27 are clearly not completely fulfilled. The third alternative is that even though we do not see a temple today, in order for this prophecy to be fulfilled, a temple <u>must</u> be built sometime in the future. The Third Temple will at least be built and in operation for sacrifices by the midpoint of the tribulation period. It could be finished one day before the midpoint, or years prior.

The interpretation that a temple will be rebuilt in the future is based on a logical deduction from the text itself and is grounded on the conviction that when God gives a prophecy, it absolutely must come to pass - or else God is a liar. Even though we might not understand the how nor think it is possible, God cannot fail. Notice what God says about prophecy in Isaiah 46:9-11, *"Remember the former things of old; for I am God, and there is no other; I am God, and there is none like me, declaring the end from the beginning and from ancient times things not yet done, saying, <u>'My counsel shall stand, and I will accomplish all my purpose,</u>' calling a bird of prey from the east, the man of my counsel from a far country. <u>I have spoken, and I will bring it</u>*

to pass; I have purposed, and I will do it." God will bring His words to pass regardless of whether we can perceive how He will see it done.

We must always take Scripture in a straightforward way when we interpret it. It is especially true when it comes to prophetic passages. Many Bible teachers in the past doubted that Israel would ever become a nation again. Instead of reading prophecy in a straightforward way, they chose to spiritualize, symbolize, or outright ignore the prophetic passages. However, those that did take it in a literal way, ended up becoming vindicated. I gave a presentation and wrote an article on this methodology that helps defend why we should approach prophecy this way. Since it was true of the prophecies concerning the first coming of Jesus, why not His second coming? You can find this article and presentation here: https://prophecywatchers.com/watching-israel. Or you can simply go to our Prophecy Watchers website and look under the "Articles" tab.

Before continuing the topic of the coming Third Temple, let me give you one more example of using logical deductions in order to understand end time prophecy. For the last 50 years, prophecy teachers have made the claim that they believed a cashless society would be coming in the end times. Why would they make such a claim? The Bible never explicitly says a cashless society is coming. Yet we have these two well-known verses, *"Also it causes all, both small and great, both rich and poor, both free and slave, to be marked on the right hand or the forehead, so that no one can buy or sell unless he has the mark, that is, the name of the beast or the number of its name"* (Revelation 13:16-17). Bible teachers deduce that in order for this to be implemented, most likely it would require a cashless or digital type currency in order to track or prevent people from buying or selling.

When this was first discussed back in the 70s, computer technology was in its infancy. Most people did not own a personal computer. Today, they are ubiquitous around the world. We call them smartphones. They are minicomputers far more advanced and sophisticated than the government computers of the 70s and 80s. Most Americans might not realize this, but there are already dozens of cashless communities in China. These are 100% cashless and digital communities. If you do not have the proper app, you cannot buy or sell in these cities. You can read more about how extensive and advanced the Chinese government is in these areas in two excellent books. One book, written in 2018 by Kai Fu Lee, is called, *Ai Superpowers: China, Silicon Valley, and the New World Order*. The other, published in October 2022 by Martin Chorzempa, is entitled, *The Cashless Revolution*. Most of what is coming as cashless will come through business and not necessarily government legislation. Some Starbucks and other stores have gone completely cashless across many of their stores. This change is just the beginning for those living in America and the rest of the Western world. All this digital technology will help make Revelation 13:16-17 come true. Bible teachers understood this over 50 years ago because they made a logical deduction from the text of Revelation. This is also true for the Third Temple and the red heifer.

    We already saw that Daniel 9:27 gives us proof that a Third Temple will be in existence in the time of the end. A second passage is given by Jesus, Himself, in the Olivet Discourse. In two places, He says something similar. Here is the Matthew version, *"So when you see the abomination of desolation spoken of by the prophet Daniel, standing in the <u>holy place</u> (let the reader understand)"* (Matthew 24:15; also Mark 13:14). The underlined phrase has two similar occurrences in the Greek New Testament (Acts 6:13; 21:28). Both of these references in the book of Acts refer to the Temple. Therefore, Jesus, as a prophet, is giving us a snapshot of a future time period when an abomination will occur in the Temple. Even though there is no Temple today, we know that one will be built in a future time in which the abomination of desolation will occur. The "abomination of desolation" phraseology appears in Daniel 9:27; 11:31; 12:11 and in the apocryphal book of 1 Maccabees 1:41-59. The Daniel 11:31 and Maccabees passages refer to an event that can only be interpreted as a real physical event that happened in the 2nd century BC. The Seleucid king Antiochus IV entered the sanctuary in 167 B.C. and desecrated it by putting an idol on the altar mixed with pig's blood (Josephus, Antiquities 12:253; 1 Maccabees 1). Both Daniel 9:27 and 12:11 are prophecies which will be fulfilled at the end of the age. Jesus intimates that what happened during the Maccabean period was a prototype of what will happen again at the end of age during the 7-year tribulation period. In order for the words of Jesus to be fulfilled, a Third Temple must be rebuilt. This is a logical deduction from the text of Scripture.

The third passage which gives solid reasoning for the future building of a Third Temple is found in 2 Thessalonians 2. Paul taught the Thessalonians extensively about the coming 7-year period ("day of the Lord") and the events leading up to its arrival. They were confused and most likely had read a false letter, allegedly from Paul, trying to convince them that the day of the Lord had arrived. Paul writes to them his 2nd letter in order to remind them of the order of events that he previously had taught them while he was with them, *"Let no one deceive you in any way. For that day will not be present, unless the rebellion comes first, and the man of lawlessness is revealed, the son of destruction, who opposes and exalts himself against every so-called god or object of worship, so that he takes his seat in the temple of God, proclaiming himself to be God. Do you not remember that when I was still with you, I told you these things?"* (2 Thessalonians 2:3-5). He reminds them that the day of the Lord (the 7-year tribulation period) will start with the rebellion (apostasy) and the man of lawlessness (antichrist) being revealed. What I think Paul is teaching is that the apostasy and the revealing of the man of lawlessness is what actually starts the day of the Lord (cf. John 5:43; Isaiah 28:15). For the Thessalonians, neither of those events had happened, so they could not be inside the day of the Lord.

Paul continues to give descriptions of what the antichrist will do once the day of the Lord starts. He will take his seat in the Temple of God proclaiming himself to be God. This desecration by the antichrist is synonymous with the abomination of desolation.

This prophetic snapshot was given to Paul at a time when the Temple was still standing. Yet it was destroyed in AD 70. Many people probably wondered what to make of Paul's prophecy since it was not fulfilled in the 1st century, becoming unable to be fulfilled without a Temple standing. We have been waiting 1900 years, but again, we must let the text mean what it says in a normal, straightforward, literal way. Now, at the end of the age we are watching the situation in Israel change right in front of our eyes. Jerusalem is now under the sovereign control of Israel. The embassy of the United States was moved to Jerusalem on May 14, 2018. The religious and political attitudes have changed dramatically in the last 15 years. We are seeing a convergence of various factors applicable to the building of the Third Temple which were not present even 20 years ago.

The final passage giving reason to believe that a physical Third Temple will be rebuilt in the last days is found in Revelation 11:1-2, *"Then I was given a measuring rod like a staff, and I was told, "Rise and measure the temple of God and the altar and those who worship there, but do not measure the court outside the temple; leave that out, for it is given over to the nations, and they will trample the holy city for forty-two months."* John is catapulted in the Spirit (Revelation 1:10; 4:2; 17:3; 21:10) to see the future. He was given several visions of the day of the Lord (7-year tribulation) which the Lord Jesus instructed him to write down and send to the seven churches of Asia minor (Revelation 1:11).

The snapshot that John saw in this section was of a physically rebuilt Temple. The angel also is a witness that there is a Temple and altar in the city of Jerusalem which is existing during the future day of the Lord. John was told to measure the Temple of God and altar. This same Greek word is used in other portions of the book of Revelation to measure something real and physical (Revelation 21:15, 16, 17). Since the Temple of God exists in the future day of the Lord, we deduce that it must be built prior to that time. It is quite reasonable to expect to see preparations to rebuild the coming Temple as we see the end of the age approaching quickly.

We have the privilege of seeing it come to fruition and to strengthen our faith. But as Jesus said, *"Blessed are those who do not see and believe"* (John 20:29). I think of William Blackstone who, in 1878, wrote his book, *Jesus is Coming*. You can find it free online. He had tremendous faith and believed that the prophecies concerning the return of the Jews to the land and the rebuilding of the Third Temple should be taken literally.

Blackstone wrote concerning the antichrist, "He will be received, even by the Jews, who, having returned to their own land and rebuilt their temple, will make a treaty with him, called by the prophet 'a covenant with death and an agreement with hell.' And antichrist will exalt himself above all that is called God, or that is worshipped, so that he as God sitteth in the temple of God (the rebuilt temple at Jerusalem) and sheweth himself that he is God" (Pp. 108-109). What amazing faith that this was written in 1878, long before the Jewish people were making any attempts at immigrating back to the land of Israel. He was confident that the Third Temple would be rebuilt because He believed the Scripture was true. And so should we.

The Bible teaches that truth should be established by two or three witnesses (Deuteronomy 19:15; Matthew 18:16; 2 Corinthians 13:1; Hebrews 10:28). God has given us four separate prophets (Daniel, Jesus, Paul, and John) to teach us that a future physical Temple will be in existence at the time of the day of the Lord. But it will not be built in one day. We should not be surprised that it will be a process that involves many layers, people, money, steps, etc. to see it all accomplished. The rest of this book will help show how the steps being taken now are unprecedented and the actual building of the Temple seems not far off.

We will get into all the details in the subsequent chapters, but for now, it might be good to simply introduce the overall requirements of what is required of the red heifers as determined by the modern rabbis who look at the Bible and their tradition. Here are the main requirements: 1) It must be a female cow. 2) It must be a red heifer that has no blemish. In other words, if it has more than two non-red hairs in one single follicle, it is disqualified. Additionally, it must not have any physical blemishes or spots. 3) It must have never been used for labor. In other words, never harnessed, or yoked. 4) It must have never been pregnant. In other words, never used as a part of the breeding program, nor have even been allowed to mate with a male cow. 5) It must be within its third year. i.e., at least one day older than two years old, but not yet four years old. 6) It must be slaughtered outside the holy city of Jerusalem but within sight of the Third Temple.

Conclusion

In summary, why should we even care about the red heifer? The main reason is that the Jewish rabbis today believe that before the Third Temple can be rebuilt, they must find and procure at least one red heifer, then slaughter the animal and obtain the ashes that will then be used for purification purposes of the priests as well as the Temple Mount itself. We will discuss and explain this more fully in the subsequent chapters, but for now it is important to recognize that whether the Jewish people are correct in thinking they need the red heifer ashes, they are determined to obtain them. In a later chapter, we will discuss the implications of the red heifer as it relates to New Testament (New Covenant) theology. In the same way that we use logical deduction to determine a Third Temple must be built, we will apply this reasoning to our thinking of the importance of the red heifer search (we will discuss the biblical basis in the next chapter). Thus, for the Jewish way of thinking, the red heifer is a pre-requisite for the actual construction of the Temple. Most, if not all, of the other preparations for the construction of Third Temple are completed - but the puzzle piece which has been missing is the acquisition of a pure red heifer. All that is changing right before our very eyes.

The fact that the red heifer hunt seems to be coming to fruition reveals to us the prophetic importance of the potential closeness of the Third Temple being rebuilt. There have been serious obstacles in the past that made the feasibility of the Third Temple being erected unrealistic. However, the religious, political, historical, logistical, and even archaeological situation has changed dramatically in the last 20 years, and even more since the beginning of 2022. We will explain all this in the remaining chapters. For now, we turn to what the Bible has to say specifically about the red heifer.

Chapter 2: The Red Heifer in the Bible

As students of the Bible, I imagine that all of us at one time or another have wished there were more details about topics that we find interesting. More specific information about the world before the flood would be helpful in understanding ancient antediluvian history. A fuller explanation of the wheels within wheels in Ezekiel 1 would be much appreciated. Exactly what were the circumstances about the saints who were raised from the dead after Jesus's resurrection (Matthew 27:52-53)? Did they die again? Did they ascend with Jesus? "Lord, can you please give us a little bit more information?" Yet God has reserved certain things to remain mysterious. Moses writes, "*The secret things belong to the Lord our God, but the things that are revealed belong to us and to our children forever, that we may do all the words of this law*" (Deuteronomy 29:29). When it comes to the slaughter of the red heifer, there are some straightforward facts, but also some interesting conundrums that are written in the text of Scripture. This is why so many books or articles talk about the mystery of the red heifer. We will explore these in the coming pages.

The Jewish rabbis today base their understanding of the red heifer ceremony on two main sources. The first is the Biblical book of Numbers 19, and the second is in the traditional sources of the Mishnah, Talmud and the Midrash commentaries. We will look at the traditional sources and what they entail in the next chapter, but for now, it would be good to examine the only place in the Old Testament where the red heifer ritual is mentioned. It will be helpful to examine the entire chapter, paragraph by paragraph, with a few comments so that we can gain an understanding of how the Jewish rabbis see this text today. We must remember that we aren't trying to assess whether we agree with their interpretations of the text, but instead how they seek to interpret and apply the text. The Jewish rabbis have thousands of years of tradition which influence their opinion. Their thinking is going to determine how they approach the building of the Third Temple and also how they feel they need to include the red heifer elements.

More important, what does Jesus the Messiah and His Father think about the building of the Third Temple? Do they approve of the efforts by the Jewish rabbis? There are a variety of opinions among modern prophecy teachers about these questions. I reached out to several well-known prophecy teachers who were gracious enough to provide their thoughts. These opinions will be addressed in a later chapter.

The Red Heifer Commandment: Numbers 19:1-22

As New Covenant (New Testament) believers, we do not often think in terms of clean and unclean. We are more inclined to focus on the concept of being forgiven or unforgiven. This perspective is accurate because we are a spiritual people and are not required to go to a physical Temple at least 3 times a year to make sacrifices as was done under the Old Covenant. *"Three times a year all your males shall appear before the LORD your God at the place that he will choose: at the Feast of Unleavened Bread, at the Feast of Weeks, and at the Feast of Booths. They shall not appear before the LORD empty-handed"* (Deuteronomy 16:16). We are purified and forever forgiven by faith through the once and for all sacrifice of Jesus (Hebrews 9:13-14; 10:1-14). Jesus also predicted that there would be a time after His departure where a physical location (and sacrifices) would not be necessary to worship the Father in spirit and in truth (John 4:21-25).

However, since modern religious Jews do not yet accept the sacrifice of Jesus for their sins, they only think in terms of the Old Testament Mosaic system and its emphasis on sacrifices within a Temple context. For them, this system does include forgiveness for sins, but it does involve the standard of being clean or unclean in a ritual sense. God had very specific instructions when approaching Him in the Tabernacle or the Temple precincts. Because the Temple will be rebuilt on the Temple Mount, they must find a way to ritually cleanse the area before they begin construction. In order to accomplish this cleansing, many believe they need the ashes from a burned (slaughtered) red heifer which will be mixed with water as outlined in Numbers 19.

Gordon Wenham, in his Tyndale Old Testament commentary on this chapter, provides a helpful introduction to the topic of uncleanness. He writes, "Leviticus prescribes two methods of dealing with uncleanness: either washing in water and waiting till evening (11:28, 39–40; 15:16–18), or in more serious cases waiting seven days and then offering a sacrifice (14:10ff.; 15:13ff., 28ff.). Offering a sacrifice was a difficult and expensive procedure, which would have greatly added to the distress of family and friends when someone died. This chapter provides an alternative remedy which marked the seriousness of the pollution caused by death, yet dealt with it without the cost and inconvenience of sacrifice. Instead, those who have come in contact with the dead can be treated with a concoction of water that contains all the ingredients of a sin offering." (p. 163, 1981). He does a great job of noting that coming into contact with a dead person was something that every person would eventually have to confront, and that God, in His grace, created an inexpensive way to become ritually clean after this happens. At the same time, there were valuable lessons in the process outlined for the red heifer which would teach His people that going from unclean to clean still required the death of an unblemished animal. A substitutionary sacrifice or slaughter involving blood was always needed to become forgiven (atonement) or to become ritually clean (Leviticus 17:11; Hebrews 9:22).

Numbers 19:1-6

"Now the Lord spoke to Moses and to Aaron, saying, 'This is the statute of the law that the Lord has commanded: Tell the people of Israel to bring you a red heifer without defect, in which there is no blemish, and on which a yoke has never come. And you shall give it to Eleazar the priest, and it shall be taken outside the camp and slaughtered before him. And Eleazar the priest shall take some of its blood with his finger, and sprinkle some of its blood toward the front of

the tent of meeting seven times. And the heifer shall be burned in his sight. Its skin, its flesh, and its blood, with its dung, shall be burned. And the priest shall take cedarwood and hyssop and scarlet yarn and throw them into the fire burning the heifer'" (Numbers 19:1-6).

The original commandment, called a "statute of the law," was given to Moses and Aaron the high priest. The non-Christian Jewish scholar Jacob Milgrom wrote a commentary on the book of Numbers for the Jewish Publication Society (JPS) in 1990, and in it he consults often with rabbinical thought. I took a course in college on Rabbinic Theology and this commentary series was highly recommended in order to gain a solid grasp of how the rabbis seek to interpret the Bible. I am sharing this not to endorse his work, but to give you an opportunity to see how modern religious Jews interpret this passage.

Milgrom writes about the word statute, "Hebrew *ḥukkat ha-torah* occurs again only in 31:21, which also begins a section on purification from corpse contamination. A similar construct, *ḥukkat ha-mishpat*, "law of procedure," is found in 27:11 and 35:29" (p. 158). We can see that the verbiage is tied to the ritual uncleanness from interacting with a dead body. This connection becomes very important later in rabbinic thinking concerning graves. There are thousands of graves, marked and unmarked, all around the Temple Mount area, including the Mount of Olives and possibly the Kidron Valley. We will examine later what the rabbis are implementing today for the ritual slaughter of the red heifer in consideration of potential uncleanness which could happen to the priests from an unmarked grave.

Another interesting thought concerning this phraseology is that Moses commanded that the people of Israel were to bring the red heifer to the high priest. It does not specify any stipulations about from where the people of Israel were to get the cow. This will become more important in discussing the rabbinic traditions that had much to say about this. Does it need to be an Israeli cow, raised in the land of Israel, or could it be purchased from Gentiles? The rabbis have an answer in their traditions, but from the Biblical text, there is nothing specific.

We learn from Milgrom that the red heifer was to be, "without blemish, in which there is no defect. This apparent redundancy is for the sake of emphasis (see Leviticus 22:21 for the identical construction). The rabbis, however, interpret 'without blemish' as referring to the color: 'unblemished red.' Hebrew 'adom, usually rendered 'red,' probably means 'brown' (for which there is no Hebrew word). Brown cows, of course, are plentiful, but one that is completely uniform in color, without specks of white or black or without even two black or white hairs, is extremely rare. Thus the rabbinic interpretation is preferred" (Milgrom, p. 158). We will see later that the rabbis are looking for cows that are redder in color rather than brown. His commentary was published in 1990 and a lot has changed since then. We should not miss the specification that the heifer was not allowed to ever be used for work (have a yoke on it). The rabbis have taken this very serious in that they seek to find a heifer that has not had anything laid on its back to the extreme. They say that even a bird landing on the back of the cow will disqualify it! The Bible does not stipulate this interpretation, but it illustrates the length the Rabbis will go in adding their tradition.

It is also essential to note that the ritual slaughter has to take place outside of the camp. In later Biblical times when the Temple was established by Solomon in Jerusalem, and even into the Second Temple period of the 1st century, we learn from rabbinic tradition that the red heifer was slaughtered and burned on the slopes of the Mount of Olives, which is east of the Temple Mount across the Kidron Valley. This is an unusual ritual in that the entire cow (including the drained blood) was to be burned. As the heifer was being burned, the priest was instructed to add cedarwood, hyssop and scarlet yarn to the fire. Milgrom writes, "…cedar wood, hyssop, and crimson stuff. The same materials were used in the purification of the leper (Leviticus 14:4, 6, 49, 51–52) and in other purification rituals throughout the ancient Near East. For example, in the Mesopotamian "Ritual … When Covering the Temple Kettle-Drum," the bull (whose hide would become the drumskin) was sprinkled with cedar balsam, burned with cedar wood, and buried in a red cloth. Since cedar, 'erez, was uncommon outside of Lebanon, some tannaim [early rabbinic teachers] and modern scholars believe that the Cyprus tree is meant. The hyssop, *'ezov*, is identified with Majorana syriaca, an aromatic plant widespread throughout the Land of Israel. Its hairy surface retains liquid and, hence, is ideal for sprinkling (v. 18; Exodus 12:22). Crimson yarn, called *tola'at shani*, literally "red dyed wool," refers to the dye extracted from a "crimson worm," the Kermes bilicus, and used in the weaving of the sacred garments of the high priest and the inner curtains of the Tabernacle (Exodus 36:8, 35, 37; 39:1–2). Shani, "crimson," seems to be an Egyptian loanword. In postexilic texts (e.g., 2 Chronicles 3:14), the term is replaced by *karmil*" (p. 159).

Interestingly, there are some, with good reason, who see a connection between the hyssop being involved here with the red heifer ritual and a hyssop branch being used to offer Jesus wine on the cross. "*A jar full of sour wine stood there, so they put a sponge full of the sour wine on a hyssop branch and held it to his mouth*" (John 19:29). It is just another insight which would point the reader of the fourth gospel back to this ceremony.

Numbers 19:7-13

"Then the priest shall wash his clothes and bathe his body in water, and afterward he may come into the camp. But the priest shall be unclean until evening. The one who burns the heifer shall wash his clothes in water and bathe his body in water and shall be unclean until evening. And a man who is clean shall gather up the ashes of the heifer and deposit them outside the camp in a clean place. And they shall be kept for the water for impurity for the congregation of the people of Israel; it is a sin offering. And the one who gathers the ashes of the heifer shall wash his clothes and be unclean until evening. And this shall be a perpetual statute for the people of Israel, and for the stranger who sojourns among them. "Whoever touches the dead body of any person shall be unclean seven days. He shall cleanse himself with the water on the third day and on the seventh day, and so be clean. But if he does not

cleanse himself on the third day and on the seventh day, he will not become clean. Whoever touches a dead person, the body of anyone who has died, and does not cleanse himself, defiles the tabernacle of the Lord, and that person shall be cut off from Israel; because the water for impurity was not thrown on him, he shall be unclean. His uncleanness is still on him" (Numbers 19:7-13).

After the ritual slaughter, the priest is required to wash his clothes and bathe because he has become unclean. We learn from verse 8 that the high priest does not need to actually be the one performing the ceremony, but simply overseeing the procedures. One of the mysteries of the red heifer ceremony is that the ritual of burning ashes, which have the ability to later cleanse people of uncleanness, actually causes uncleanness itself to those performing the service. This ritual is not simply for Israel, but for any foreigner who has chosen to live in Israel under the Mosaic covenant.

Once the ritual ceremony was completed, the ashes were to be kept safe. Milgrom writes, "to be kept, rather, 'to be safeguarded.' The ashes of the red cow must be guarded scrupulously lest they become invalidated through contamination. During Second Temple times the ashes were divided into three parts: one-third for sprinkling, one-third for sanctifying new lustral water, and one-third for safekeeping" (p. 160).

God then gives specific instructions for Moses and the people of Israel about how to use the ashes of the red heifer when mixed with water in order to clean someone of uncleanness. The unclean person must be sprinkled with the new water on the third and seventh days (v.12). If the person does not follow this exactly, the person defiles the Tabernacle or Temple of the Lord and will be cut off from the people of God. This is a very serious situation and why God has created the ceremony to produce the red heifer ashes. Milgrom writes, "The demand for purification from corpse contamination was so great during Second Temple times that the purificatory waters were made available in twenty-four districts of the country. Even after the destruction of the Temple these waters were still available in Judea, Galilee, Transjordan, and Ezion-geber (Assia) in the south." (p. 161).

Numbers 19:14-22

"*This is the law when someone dies in a tent: everyone who comes into the tent and everyone who is in the tent shall be unclean seven days. And every open vessel that has no cover fastened on it is unclean. Whoever in the open field touches someone who was killed with a sword or who died naturally, or touches a human bone or a grave, shall be unclean seven days. For the unclean they shall take some ashes of the burnt sin offering, and fresh water shall be added in a vessel. Then a clean person shall take hyssop and dip it in the water and sprinkle it on the tent and on all the furnishings and on the persons who were there and on whoever touched the bone, or the slain or the dead or the grave. And the clean person shall sprinkle it on the unclean on the third day and on the seventh day. Thus on the seventh day he shall cleanse him, and he shall wash his clothes and bathe himself in water, and at evening he shall be clean. "If the man who is unclean does not cleanse himself, that person shall be cut off from the midst of the assembly, since he has defiled the sanctuary of the Lord. Because the water for impurity has not been thrown on him, he is unclean. And it shall be a statute forever for them. The one who sprinkles the water for impurity shall wash his clothes, and the one who touches the water for impurity shall be unclean until evening. And whatever the unclean person touches shall be unclean, and anyone who touches it shall be unclean until evening*" (Numbers 19:14-22).

      This section is straightforward and gives stipulations for when a person dies inside a tent. This was a common occurrence, especially during the 40-year wilderness wandering when that entire generation died off. In verse 17, we read about blending the water and the ashes of the red heifer in a vessel in order to create a mixture which could be sprinkled on the tent and persons. Milgrom writes, "The text implies that the water was added to the ashes. The rabbis, however, held that the ashes were added to the water. Perhaps the ashes were held in a porous cloth through which the water was filtered" (p. 162). This practice was an important thought and tradition by the rabbis. Because they chose to interpret the text as saying the ashes were added to water instead of water to ashes in a vessel, they were able to exponentially expand the volume of mixed ashes and water available to be kept for the people. This also allowed them to create gigantic stores of the mixture which could be transported and kept continuous for generations.

As you can see from examining the Biblical text, there are certainly very specific stipulations, but there is not an extensive number of regulations explained. The text does not get into all the details of the why or even the how, but simply a general overview. It makes sense why the rabbis spent much time throughout the ages trying to come up with interpretations which made the non-explicit, explicit. They did not want to offend God and so they had friendly arguments back and forth about the extreme details which we will cover in the next chapter.

Why should we care about the nitty gritty of rabbinic historical thought concerning the red heifer? In some ways, one could argue that we really do not need to care that much. The Bible says a Temple will be rebuilt and that is all we should care about. That is one perspective that might be satisfactory to some, but I take a different outlook.

God calls the day of the Lord a time of intense trouble. *"The great day of the Lord is near, near and hastening fast; the sound of the day of the Lord is bitter; the mighty man cries aloud there. A day of wrath is that day, a day of distress and anguish, a day of ruin and devastation, a day of darkness and gloom, a day of clouds and thick darkness, a day of trumpet blast and battle cry against the fortified cities and against the lofty battlements. I will bring distress on mankind, so that they shall walk like the blind, because they have sinned against the Lord; their blood shall be poured out like dust, and their flesh like dung. Neither their silver nor their gold shall be able to deliver them on the day of the wrath of the Lord. In the fire of his jealousy, all the earth shall be consumed; for a full and sudden end he will make of all the inhabitants of the earth"* (Zephaniah 1:14-18). Even more serious is that God says through Jeremiah, *"Alas! That day is so great there is none like it; it is a time of distress for Jacob; yet he shall be saved out of it*" (Zephaniah 30:7).

The Jewish people believe that the earthly kingdom is coming through the arrival of the Messiah. This is true, but before it does, God is going to have a serious talk with them about their rejection and killing of Jesus the Messiah. God will use the 7-year day of the Lord to discipline them into a state of repentance and acknowledgement of their sin of piercing their Messiah (cf. Zechariah 12:10). We know that by the end of the tribulation, the persecution will be so severe that they will call upon the name of Jesus to rescue them from the antichrist and worldwide persecution meant to bring genocide on the Jews. Jesus said that the Jewish people would not see Him again until they receive Him. "*O Jerusalem, Jerusalem, the city that kills the prophets and stones those who are sent to it! How often would I have gathered your children together as a hen gathers her brood under her wings, and you were not willing! See, your house is left to you desolate. For I tell you, you will not see me again, until you say, 'Blessed is he who comes in the name of the Lord'*" (Matthew 23:37-39).

What this passage reveals is that many of the religious Jewish people currently believe that they need to build a Temple to please God so as to draw closer to Him. In order to do this, they must also follow the prescriptions of Numbers 19 and perform the ritual slaughter of the red heifer in order to obtain the ashes and cleanse the Temple Mount area in preparation for the construction of the Third Temple. The rabbis have come to outline extremely detailed specifications in order to make this happen. Some of these criteria are extremely difficult to recreate, but through the providence of God, He is allowing them to come to fruition. Why? Because God's ultimate goal is to save the Jewish people (Romans 11:26). He knows that in order to get them focused on Him, they will need to sacrifice the red heifer, build the Temple, and then be put under serious distress as Jeremiah 30:7 shows. Then and only then will their hearts be humbled to receive and call out to Jesus at the end of the tribulation period (Hosea 5:15).

In the next chapter, we will examine the fine details of rabbinic thought concerning the red heifer. We will also be able to recognize that, as extreme and stringent as these technicalities are, they are beginning to be able to be fulfilled in our time after a hiatus of almost 2000 years. The more outlandish it is to have all of them converge at the same time, the more amazing it is to realize that we are living in the time of the fulfillment of these items!

Do not forget that the ultimate point is not simply to be amazed at prophecy, but to ask yourself whether you are spiritually ready for the Lord's return at the rapture.

Chapter 3: The Red Heifer in Rabbinic Tradition

Let me just say up front that this chapter can only end up being a basic summary of the very wide and complex world of rabbinic tradition. It is necessary because the rabbis today who are seeking and preparing for the slaughter of the red heifer are basing their requirements not just on the Bible, but on the various traditions that have been handed to them from the previous 2000 years. As we ponder these prophetic developments, some questions come up which contribute to what we are observing in Israel today. All the following questions are discussed in the rabbinical writings.
1) How old does the heifer need to be before it is slaughtered?
2) How many non-red hairs can the cow have before it becomes disqualified?
3) Is there a location where the heifer needs to be burned?
4) Is it okay if the heifer is not raised in Israel, or can it be purchased from the Gentiles?

I have studied rabbinic theology for over 20 years, and sometimes it can be quite laborious! If you are not that interested, feel free to skim the following survey. Not everybody is drawn into getting into the minutia of the large body of literature that we know as rabbinic tradition. For those interested in getting into the details, this will be an overview that will provide original source material to which most people often do not have access. There definitely are many correlations between Jesus and the oral traditions, as well as in other parts of the New Testament.

One of the best ways to learn more about rabbinic tradition is through the free basic edition of Logos software. They also have for free the *Lexham Bible Dictionary* which I highly recommend. In order to keep it simple and to direct you to something you can check out on your own, the following is from that dictionary under "Rabbinic Literature and the New Testament" with some of my explanations in parentheses:

Rabbinic literature is a body of literature composed by Jewish sages who examined the written Scripture in light of the oral Torah.

These writings can broadly be divided into two parts: 1) literature centered on the law; and 2) literature dedicated to the theology and exposition of the Old Testament. The part of rabbinic literature centered on the law is specifically focused on halakha (Jewish religious laws), and some of the texts in this part include:

- the Mishnah (the written oral Torah - around AD 200)
- the Tosefta (similar to Mishnah and seen as a supplement to the Mishnah. Written around the same time as the Mishnah)
- the two Talmuds: Jerusalem (the Talmud of the land of Israel finalized between AD 350-400) and Bavli (the Talmud collated in Babylon - finalized AD 500)
- Exodus: Mekhilta (All these below are basically commentaries in a general sense)
- Leviticus: Sifra
- Sifré to Numbers
- Sifré to Deuteronomy

Some rabbinic works committed to the theology and exposition of the Old Testament include:

- Genesis Rabbah
- Leviticus Rabbah
- Pesiqta deRab Kahana
- Lamentations Rabbah
- Song of Songs Rabbah
- Ruth Rabbah
- Esther Rabbah **(end of *Lexham Dictionary* excerpt)**

The rabbis believe that God gave Moses the written Torah (also called the Pentateuch) - the first five books of the Old Testament). Although there is no specific evidence to support it, the rabbis remain steadfast in their belief that God also gave Moses the oral Torah (which is the proper interpretation of the written Word). This oral tradition is said to have been passed down through the various scribes, priests, or prophets - from Moses (about 1400 BC) all the way to AD 200 when this oral tradition was finally written down by Judah ha Nasi in what is called the Mishnah. We read from the New Testament that in the time of Jesus, the oral tradition, "tradition of the Elders," was in existence. For a Jewish rabbi, this tradition has just as much authority as the written Word. For Christians and other Jews (known as Karaite Jews), we do not believe that the oral Torah or tradition has the same level of absolute authority as the Bible. In the gospels, we see that Jesus referenced the tradition of the elders on several occasions. He never quoted it as an authority and in some instances, he rebuked the Pharisees for allowing their traditions to be followed as equal with or to take away from the written word of God.

Mark writes, "*And the Pharisees and the scribes asked him, "Why do your disciples not walk according to the <u>tradition of the elders</u>, but eat with defiled hands?" And He said to them, "Well did Isaiah prophesy of you hypocrites, as it is written, "'This people honors Me with their lips, but their heart is far from Me; in vain do they worship Me, <u>teaching as doctrines the commandments of men</u>.' You leave <u>the commandment of God and hold to the tradition of men."</u> And He said to them, "You have a fine way of rejecting the commandment of God in order to establish your tradition! For Moses said, 'Honor your father and your mother'; and, 'Whoever reviles father or mother must surely die.' But you say, 'If a man tells his father or his mother, "Whatever you would have gained from me is Corban"' (that is, dedicated to God)-- then you no longer permit him to do anything for his father or mother, thus making void the word of God by <u>your tradition that you have handed down</u>. And many such things you do*" (Mark 7:5-13). We learn that this tradition became an obstacle at times for the Pharisees to follow the written Word. The simple fact is that Jesus made a strong distinction between the written authoritative Word of God and the non-authoritative traditions of the elders.

Does this mean that every last part of the Jewish tradition is wrong? Not at all. In fact, much of their efforts were intended to keep people from sinning. They would take a well-known law of the written Word, let's say adultery, and they would add new laws ("fences") around the written Mosaic law to help keep a person from sinning. These fences became part of the oral law or traditions. For example, the Mishnah (Kiddushin 4:12) says, "A man may not be alone with two women, but one woman may be alone with two men." It also says, in 4:14, "Whoever has business with women should not be alone with women." When you go to Israel today and interact with many of the ultra-orthodox Jewish men, often you will see them be completely dismissive of a woman stranger in their presence. We often interpret this as being rude and sometimes it might be. Yet for them, the oral tradition gives the above commandments, and so if they follow these, they will never commit adultery and break the written commandment. They have built a fence around the law. Think of it like a cliff and falling off the edge as committing adultery. If you build a fence twenty feet back from the cliff and never cross the fence, you will never even come close to falling off the cliff (i.e., commit adultery). That is part of their logic.

The Mishnah (and Tosefta) are arranged with six major divisions (called orders). These summations of religious oral law cover a variety of topics. They include seeds (agricultural rules), festivals, women, damages, holy things, and purity laws. There are many subchapters to each of these orders.

The Talmud, as a body of literature, can appear in printed editions up to 38 volumes! It is huge and requires a great amount of study in order to be fluent. The Talmud has two different editions as mentioned above, the Jerusalem and the Babylonian. Both follow a similar organizational structure based on the Mishnah. These Talmuds have two parts. The first paragraph of a section is a reprinting of the actual text of the Mishnah (AD 200), and then what follows on the page is called the Gemara. The Gemara is a commentary and analysis of the Mishnah by various rabbis up to around AD 400. The Talmud is thought to have been finished around AD 500.

When it comes to the ritual slaughter of the red heifer being prepared in our current day, the rabbis have consulted the Bible (Numbers 19) and all the various traditions over the last 2000 years. Of the hundreds of different topics that appear in the Mishnah, there is a specific chapter on the red heifer ceremony. In the sixth order, there is a subchapter called Parah - which is the Hebrew word for cow. We cannot cover every last detail, but a few become very important, especially as we try to ascertain the prophetic implications that are coming to fruition in the present era.

Remember, these are exciting times! God is providentially allowing these events to come to pass in preparation for the arrival of the 7-year tribulation period and eventually the return of Jesus. None of these items are coincidences. Though we must be prepared spiritually at all times, things do seem to be moving extremely fast over the last couple of years and are accelerating.

Now that we have done a short summary of the rabbinical writings, we can revisit the original questions that were stated at the front of this chapter.

1) How old does the heifer need to be before it is slaughtered?
2) How many non-red hairs can the cow have before it becomes disqualified?
3) Is there a location where the heifer needs to be burned?
4) Is it okay if the heifer is not raised in Israel or can it be purchased from the Gentiles?

How old must the red heifer be in order to be slaughtered?

Here we can be reminded of the well-known witticism, "When two Jews are present, you have three opinions." This is so true, and even Jewish people joke about this stereotype. It also becomes evident if you spend any time in the rabbinical writings. As we examine some of these questions in the rabbinical literature below, we will realize that we cannot have a definitive answer. Many of the various rabbis give differing opinions and arguments for theological viewpoints. You can observe this in the following section of the Parah chapter from the Mishnah about how old the heifer should be.

1:1   A   Rabbi Eliezer says, "A heifer—a year old.
       B   "And a cow—two years old."
       C   1. And sages say, "A heifer—two years old, and a cow—three years old,

		2. "or four years old."
	D	Rabbi Meir says, "Even one five years old.
	E	1. The old one is suitable.
		2. But they do not keep it waiting, lest a hair turn black [and] it should not [otherwise] become unfit."
	F	Said Rabbi Joshua, "I heard only shelashit [the third]."
	G	They said to him, "What is the meaning of the language, shelashit [the third]?"
	H	Said he to them, "Thus I have heard plain [without explanation]."
	I	Said Ben Azzai, "I shall explain.
	J	"If you say shelishit, [it means the third in relationship] to others in sequence.
	K	"And when you say shelashit, [it means] three years old."
1:2	A	Rabbi Yose the Galilean says, "Bullocks — two years old.
	B	"As it is said, And a second [year] bullock of the herd you take for a purification offering (Numbers 8:8)."
	C	And sages say, "Even one three years old."
	D	Rabbi Meir says, "Even one four years old,
	E	"even one five years old are suitable.
	F	"But they do not bring old ones, because of the honor [of the altar]."¹

As you can see from the above quote of the actual Mishnah text, there are various opinions of the rabbis through the centuries. Some say one, two, three, four, or five years old. So, what is the final opinion? In Israel today there are various religious factions which often disagree with each other. Even among the ultra-orthodox Jewish groups you will find various commentary and judicial requirements. Rabbi Chaim Richman of the Temple Institute wrote a book in 1997 entitled, "The Mystery of the Red Heifer." He is still active and

---

¹ Jacob Neusner, *The Mishnah : A New Translation* (New Haven, CT: Yale University Press, 1988), 1012.

considered the premier authority in the matters of rebuilding the Temple. On page 21 of that book, he mentions that Rabbi Eliezer (a very esteemed rabbi of the 1st and 2nd century AD and quoted above in 1:1B) believed that the red heifer needed to be 2 years old. Yet Rabbi Richman says that Rabbi Meir's judgment of 3 years old is the consensus accepted today by the majority of the rabbis. Yet how one defines 3 years old also is debated.

    The well-known ancient Targum Pseudo-Jonathan (an Aramaic translation of the Pentateuch) translates Numbers 19:2 in this way, *"This is the decree, the publication of the law which the Lord hath commanded, saying: Speak to the sons of Israel, that they bring to thee from the separation of the fold a red heifer, <u>two years old</u>, in which there is neither spot nor white hair, on which no male hath come, nor the burden of any work been imposed, neither hurt by the thong, nor grieved by the goad or prick, nor collar (band) or any like yoke."* This passage provides another ancient source of understanding that a two-year-old heifer is the appropriate age. Nevertheless, the modern rabbinic consensus has a divergent view.

    What does this mean for our current situation? There have been several potential red heifers through the years. Beginning in the 1990s, several candidates have started out with good possibilities, and then later became disqualified by growing non-red hairs. The consensus ruling comes into focus when discussing the 5 red heifers from a ranch in Texas that were flown to Israel and landed on September 15, 2022. These heifers were born around October 5, 2021. This date becomes very important when thinking of the prophetic significance of the time when they will become eligible to be slaughtered. Even though we know the relatively close birth date of this group of 5 heifers, there still can be confusion as to how old they must be according to Jewish tradition. In my research, I have heard from credible sources that the rabbis believe they need to be at least 2 years and 8 days old, and up to 3 years and 8 days old. The present consensus seems to be 2 years and 1 month old (the third year). This contributes to how we look at the calendar in the coming months concerning the current group of 5 that were flown at considerable expense to Israel. If we take the minimum age, then this coming October, 2023, at least one will become eligible to be slaughtered in the red heifer ritual. Recently, it has been publicly stated by the group *Boneh Israel* that they hope that they will be ready for ritual slaughter during Passover of 2024 (April 5-13, 2024) or during the Fall Festivals 2024.

The Temple Institute has stated quite vocally that even if these current 5 heifers do not qualify at the proper age, they have arrangements with several ranchers who are producing other red heifers to send to Israel. There are also additional breeders who are breeding the red heifers inside the land of Israel. They have not and will not give up on trying to fulfill this requirement for the building of the Third Temple.

How many non-red hairs will disqualify the heifer?

Just like we saw in the previous question, there are various opinions and answers within groups today. The Bible teaches that it must be a red cow and does not give specifics of what that exactly means. This is where the rabbis through the centuries have sought to make explicit what is not made explicit in the text of Scripture. Their opinions are recorded in the Mishnah and the Babylonian Talmud. Notice first the variation in opinions as related in the Parah chapter of the Mishnah:

2:5   A   [If] there were on it two black hairs, or white ones, inside a single follicle, it is unfit.
      B   R. Judah says, "Even in one hollow."
      C   [If] they were in two hollows, and they are opposite [adjacent to] one another—it is unfit.
      D   R. Aqiba says, "Even four, even five, and they are scattered about—let one uproot them."
      E   R. Eliezer says, "Even fifty."
      F   R. Joshua b. Beterah says, "Even one on its head and one on its tail—it is unfit."

G	There were on it two hairs—
H	their root is black and their head is red—
I	their root is red and their head is black—
J	"All follows that which is seen," the words of R. Meir.
K	And sages say, "[All follows the condition of] the root."[2]

In the Talmud there are similar discussions and ambiguity. It reads:

O.	If there were on a red cow two black hairs or white ones in one follicle, it is unfit; in two follicles—it is fit. R. Judah says, "Even in two follicles and they are adjacent to one another, it is unfit." If there were on it two hairs, with a red root and a black head, R. Yosé b. Hammeshullam says, "One shaves the top and does not reckon with the possibility that he is liable on account of shearing the red cow" [Talmud Babylonia, Parah 2:7A–E].[3]

As you can read, there is not a single consensus in either the Mishnah or the Talmud. Some of the rabbis even say that it is ok to pluck out some of the non-red hairs in order to maintain that it is keeping its red color. There are several articles on the Temple Institute website pertaining to the red heifer. At that site, they write, *"The heifer must be three years old and perfect in its redness. This means that the presence of as few as two hairs of any other color from a single follicle (or two that are in adjacent follicles) will render it invalid; it is related that for this reason, the red heifer was always very expensive to procure. Even its hooves must be red. It must also be totally free from any physical blemish or defect, whether internal or external."* There is no doubt that the Temple Institute is the leading group in determining what is

---

[2] Jacob Neusner, *The Mishnah : A New Translation* (New Haven, CT: Yale University Press, 1988), 1015.
[3] Jacob Neusner, *The Babylonian Talmud: A Translation and Commentary*, vol. 21a (Peabody, MA: Hendrickson Publishers, 2011), 114.

accepted in the community. For them, even two non-red hairs from a single follicle will disqualify the cow. Others say that two non-red hairs are ok, so I imagine more will be revealed as we get closer to the date.

One of the most influential rabbis in history was a Spanish Jew named Moses ben Maimon, who lived from AD 1138-1204. He is generally known as Maimonides (or Rambam). He wrote a massive 14 volume tome called the *Mishneh Torah* which was a treatise on Jewish law taking into consideration the various influential Jewish writers from the time of the Talmud (AD 500) up until his own time. His opinions carry great weight today and I include them here for easy access. He gives his opinion on the back-and-forth decisions concerning how many non-red hairs are allowed. He leans towards a commonsense approach in that the most important determining factor is whether the roots are red. Maimonides wrote this over 1000 years after the Second Temple was destroyed, but he longed for the time when the Temple would be rebuilt and provided a framework for this to happen. The following is from chapter one of his book on the red heifer topic. He writes,

> "Included in this text are two positive commandments. They comprise the following:
> 1) the laws of the red heifer; 2) the laws of the impurity and purity brought about by the water used for the sprinkling of its ashes. These mitzvot [commandments] are explained in the ensuing chapters.
>
> **1** The commandment involving the red heifer is to offer such an animal in its third or fourth year of life. If it is older, it is acceptable, but we do not wait for it to age longer, lest its hairs become black.
> The Jewish community does not purchase a calf and raise it, for Numbers 19:2 states: "And you shall take unto yourselves a heifer," i.e., a heifer, not a calf. If only a calf was found, a price is established for it and it should remain in its owner's

possession until it matures and becomes a cow. It should be purchased with money from the Temple treasury.

2 The Torah's description of this heifer as "perfect" means "perfectly red," not perfect in stature. Even if it is dwarf size, it is acceptable, as is the law regarding other sacrifices. If it had two white hairs or black hairs growing from one follicle or from two cavities and they are lying on top of each other, it is unacceptable.

3 If there were two hairs, their roots reddish and their heads blackish, or their roots blackish and their heads reddish, their status follows the roots entirely. One should cut off the blackish head with scissors. He need not be concerned about the prohibition against shearing consecrated animals, because his intention is not to shear.

4 Enough of the red hair must remain so that it can be pulled out by tweezers. For if a hair is not large enough to be pulled out by tweezers, it is considered as if it does not exist. Therefore, if there were two white or black hairs that are so small that they cannot be pulled out by tweezers, it is acceptable.

5 If its horns or hooves are black, they may be cut off and it is acceptable. The color of the eyeballs, the teeth, and the tongue do not disqualify a heifer."

You can find the full work of Maimonides at the following link. <https://www.chabad.org/library/article_cdo/aid/1517250/jewish/Parah-Adumah.htm>. The important thing to note is that once again the final conclusion as to how many non-red hairs will be accepted could change. There are strong opinions by various groups, but each group has an ancient source to make an appeal and depending on how desperate the situation becomes, they easily could change from the current consensus.

Where is the location the red heifer is supposed to be slaughtered?

The short answer is on the Mount of Olives, which is east of the Temple Mount and across the Kidron Valley of Jerusalem. This is where we are reminded that we are living in the age of fulfilled prophecy and even more prophecy to come. Israel became a nation in 1948 and gained control of eastern Jerusalem (which includes the Mount of Olives) in 1967. Without these miraculous events of history there would be no way to prepare for the coming of the Third Temple and slaughter of the red heifer. We do not need to question where the slaughter of the red heifer took place. The Mishnah (AD 200) says it quite clearly in the Parah chapter:

3:6　　A　　And they would make a causeway from the Temple Mount to the Mount of Olives, arches upon arches, an arch directly above each pair,
　　　　　B　　because of the grave in the depths,
　　　　　C　　on which the priest who burns the cow, and the cow, and all those that assist it go forth to the Mount of Olives.[4]

I encourage you to check out the Temple Institute website and its pages on the red heifer. They have some great artistic renderings of the entire ceremony, and also of the priests and the other regulations. As we read above in the Mishnah, there was a causeway from the Temple Mount across the Kidron valley to the proper location of the ritual slaughter. You can see a great drawing at this web address <https://templeinstitute.org/red-heifer-the-ceremony/>. In the

---

[4] Jacob Neusner, *The Mishnah : A New Translation* (New Haven, CT: Yale University Press, 1988), 1016.

picture and as written in the Mishnah, it is noted that the causeway was held up by arches. This observation leads to interesting rabbinic thinking concerning graves.

We saw earlier from Numbers 19:16-18 that God instructed that anyone who came into contact with a dead person or a grave would become ritually unclean. The rabbis took this literally and sought to come up with ways to make sure that priests would not become unclean just in case they inadvertently walked over an unmarked grave. How could they guarantee this? There were two main considerations. One would be to always walk on bedrock. The nature of bedrock would inherently prohibit the possibility that a grave could exist under the bedrock. The second was that if you built an elevated path with empty space between the elevated walkway and the ground, you would not become contaminated as there is a separation of empty space between the ground and the walkway.

For this reason, the Mishnah records that the causeway built from the Temple Mount had arches. The arched causeway would automatically guarantee that they could not become contaminated or unclean by coming into contact with a grave as they made their way from the Temple Mount to the location of the ritual slaughter of the red heifer. We see this reasoning in the Mishnah (above) and also later in Maimonides's teachings. He writes in chapter 3 of the *Mishneh Torah* about the location,

> **1** The red heifer should be burnt only outside the Temple Mount, as Numbers 19:3 states: *"And you shall take it outside the camp."* They would burn it on the Mount of Olives. A ramp was built from the Temple Mount to the Mount of Olives. Below it were arches upon arches, i.e., an arch on two arches, so that there would be empty space under it, lest there be a grave in the depths of the earth. Similarly, the place where the heifer was burnt and the place of immersion on the Mount of Olives had the space under them hollowed, lest there be a grave in the depths of the earth. The red heifer, the one who

would burn it, and all those who assist in its burning go from the Temple Mount to the Mount of Olives on this ramp.

2 How was the red heifer burnt? The elders of Israel would walk to the Mount of Olives first. There was a mikveh there. The priest, those assisting in burning it, and the heifer would go out on the ramp and come to the Mount of Olives.

When it comes to the modern era, we can learn a few things about what the rabbis have been doing in preparing the slaughter of the red heifer. The above information reveals that it must be on the Mount of Olives and is said to need to be in line of sight with the Temple building. This means that for the line of sight to be maintained, the location must be up the slope of the Mount of Olives at least a minimum amount. It cannot be down in the Kidron valley.

Boneh Israel is a non-profit organization in Israel. Their website describes their purpose as: *"Boneh Israel (literally: "Building Israel") is a nonprofit organization focused on building up and reviving important Biblical sites, bringing the Bible to life, educating the nations about the past, present and future of Israel, and actively bringing the redemption closer."* This organization purchased property on the Mount of Olives back in 2011, northeast of the Church of All Nations where people can visit their garden of Gethsemane. Right now, this site is the main site promoted by Boneh Israel and the Temple Institute. I had an opportunity to interview Byron Stinson who is the American leader of Boneh Israel. On the following map you will see the location of the property they purchased in which they plan to move forward with the ritual slaughter in spring of 2024.

Another site on the map that has been proposed was just west (and below) the Dominus Flevit Church on the slopes of the Mount of Olives. This piece of property has an excellent line of sight onto the Temple Mount and is a good candidate for the location of a future red heifer burning ceremony. Based on some information presented by Joseph Good on his Facebook page, this is claimed to be one of the options for the location of the ritual slaughter of the red heifer.

EAST

Russian Ascension Tower

MOUNT OF OLIVES

Dome of the Ascension

Boneh Israel
Red Heifer Ritual Site

Dominus Flevit Church

Flevit
Red Heifer Ritual Site

Temple Axis Line
6.5° North of East

KIDRON VALLEY

Golden Gate

TEMPLE MOUNT

Herodian Temple

Dome of the Rock (octagon)

NORTH

SOUTH

WEST

Once again, we realize that so many of the puzzle pieces are coming together. There certainly is a convergence of details that are being arranged and secured in advance so that when a red heifer becomes available, there will not be any hindrances to performing the ritual. These recent developments were still only a dream not too long ago. Think of living in 1947 or 1966 when the religious Jews around the world did not have any concrete hope that their vision of a new temple and the reinstitution of a red heifer slaughter would be realized. All that has changed in the current time. As Dr. Arnold Fruchtenbaum says, the footsteps of the Messiah are indeed being heard in our current day!

Is it okay if the heifer is not raised in Israel or can it be purchased from Gentiles (non-Jews)?

This question actually has some fascinating history and some uncanny connections to the modern situation of the newly acquired 5 red heifers sent to Israel from Texas in September, 2022. First, we can see that the Mishnah (Parah) has something to say about this question.

2:1	A	R. Eliezer says, "A cow for purification which is pregnant is suitable."
	B	And sages declare unfit.
	C	R. Eliezer says, "**It is not purchased from the gentiles.**"
	D	And sages declare fit.
	E	And not this alone, but:
	F	All community and private offerings derive from the Land and from abroad,
	G	from what is new and from what is old [produce],
	H	except for the *omer* and two bread [loaves, Leviticus 23:17],
	I	which come only from what is new and from the land.

This passage in the Mishnah quotes Rabbi Eliezer, who rules that the red heifer cannot be purchased from Gentiles. However, this is not the final consensus today. When we examine the position of Maimonides, he addresses this issue and writes in *Mishneh Torah* 1:7: "All of the physical blemishes that disqualify sacrificial animals, also disqualify a red heifer, for the prooftext cited above states: 'Which does not possess a blemish.' If the heifer was born by Caesarian section, was exchanged for a dog, was a present given a prostitute, was *treifah*, or had been sodomized, it is unacceptable. For any factor that invalidates a sacrificial animal for the altar invalidates the red heifer even though it is considered only as consecrated for the upkeep of the Temple, for Scripture has called it a sin-offering. **It is permitted to purchase a red heifer from a gentile**. We do not suspect that the gentile sodomized it, for he would not destroy the value of his animal."

The general agreement today is that it is allowed to purchase a red heifer cow from Gentiles. In fact, this becomes obvious in that the five red heifers that arrived in Israel on September 15, 2022, were purchased from a rancher in Texas for a significant amount of money. I will share some interesting details about the modern story, but before we do there is a fascinating story in the rabbinic tradition discussing this exact question.

The Jerusalem Talmud (among other rabbinical literature) notes how a Gentile was praised for his honor to his father while he was sleeping. This story is found in Kiddushin (Qiddushin) 1:7.

II:3 [A] To what extent does the requirement of honoring the father and mother extend?

[B] He [Eleazar, Y. Pe. 1:1] said to them, "Are you asking me? Go and ask Damah son of Netinah. He was the chief of the *patroboule* of his town. One time his mother was slapping him before the entire council, and the slipper she was beating him with fell from her hand, and he got down and gave it back to her, so that she would not be upset."

[C] Said Rabbi Hezekiah, "He was a gentile from Ashkelon, and head of the *patroboule* of his town. Now if there was a stone on which his father had sat, he would never sit on it. When [his father] died, he made the stone into his god."

[D] One time the <u>Benjamin-jewel</u> in the high priest's breastplate was lost [cf. Jastrow, p. 601]. *They said, "Who has one as fine as that one? They said that Damah son of Netinah had one. They went to him and made a deal with him to buy it for a hundred denars. He went to get it for them, and he found that his father was sleeping [on the box containing the jewel].*

[E] *And some say that the key to the box was on the finger of his father, and some say that his foot was stretched out over the jewel cask.*

[F] *He went down to them and said, "I can't bring it to you." They said, "Perhaps it is because he wants more money." They raised the price to two hundred, then to a thousand. Once his father woke up from his sleep, he went up and got the jewel for them.*

[G] *They wanted to pay him what they had offered at the end, but he would not accept the money from them. He said, "Shall I sell you [at a price] the honor I pay to my father? I shall not derive benefit by reason of the honor I pay to my father."*

[H] How did the Holy One, blessed be he, reward him?

[I] Said R. Yosé b. R. Bun, "That very night his cow produced a <u>red cow</u>, and the Israelites paid him its weight in gold and weighed for use for producing purification water in line with[5]

What can we learn from this story? Actually, there are several things that correlate to what we observe, and which have shaped the thinking of many rabbis today. If you want the full source list for this story and how it appears in various writings you can find it at this website: <https://www.encyclopedia.com/religion/encyclopedias-almanacs-transcripts-and-maps/dama-son-netina>.

In particular, there are two important details that stand out. The first is that the ancient Jews were looking to restore the jewel representing the tribe of Benjamin that needed replacing for the breastplate of the high priest. Second, they went to a Gentile man to buy the jewel and he showed great honor to his father. In reward for honoring his father, God blessed this Gentile with a red heifer cow which he also sold to the Israelites to fulfill their need.

I will give more details later about the five red heifers that were flown to Israel in September 2022, but the Christian owner of the ranch who sold these cows is named Ty Davenport. He owns and runs a ranch called Triple Creek Ranch. You can find his website at <triplecreekredangus.com>. Interestingly, his brother, Brian Davenport, was very instrumental in connecting the Israeli rabbis with his rancher brother, Ty. Why is this interesting? Well, would you believe that Brian Davenport is a diamond jeweler who has traveled to all parts of the world including Israel to sell jewels?

You can see why the rabbis are extremely excited. They approached a jeweler, who in turn introduced them to his brother, from whom they were able to acquire 5 red heifers. Very similar to the

---

R. Rabbi
b. *ben,* son (of)
R. Rabbi
[5] Jacob Neusner, *The Jerusalem Talmud: A Translation and Commentary* (Peabody, Massachusetts: Hendrickson Publishers, 2008).

traditional story of Damah ben (son of) Netinah. What does this prove? Nothing exactly, but it is one of those stories which includes some uncanny similarities and coincidences. These are the tiny elements which help the rabbis believe that God is guiding their steps in order to procure a red heifer in order to hasten the building of the Third Temple.

Does God really approve of their efforts? Is God helping them find a red heifer? I will address this topic in a subsequent chapter, but I bring this up to simply show how the rabbis are interpreting these events. They are convinced that God is working out these little miracles and providential provisions to support their efforts of a red heifer acquisition.

There is one last rabbinic belief that is worthy of being brought up in this chapter. Based on the previous story and many others, the rabbis are convinced that we are living in the age of the Messiah's arrival. And so are we as prophecy watchers! Yet there is a big difference in what we think is going to happen at the end of the age versus their belief. We believe Jesus is going to be returning a 2nd time to rapture His church, judge the world, chasten the nation Israel, and come back in full glory to destroy the antichrist and his system, and then establish His 1000-year Messianic kingdom after redeeming a repentant Israel.

The religious Jews believe that indeed the Messiah will come back, but it will be his first time and they will see him establish and provide a red heifer and the building of the temple to restore the Mosaic covenant and its sacrificial system.

The Mishnah, written around AD 200, records a history of how many red heifers have been slaughtered since the time of Moses. It reads:

3:5　　A　　"[If] they did not find [the residue of the ash] from seven [former cows of purification], they did it from six, from five, from four, from three, from two, from one.

　　　　　B　　"And who prepared them?

C	"The first did Moses prepare. And the second did Ezra prepare.
D	"And five from Ezra onward," the words of R. Meir.
E	And sages say, "Seven from Ezra onward.
F	"And who prepared them?
G	"Simeon the Righteous and Yohanan the High Priest did two each. Elyehoenai b. Haqqof and Hanamel the Egyptian, and Ishmael b. Phiabi did one each."[6]

Maimonides also contributes to the discussion when he writes in the *Mishneh Torah* 3:4, "Nine red heifers were offered from the time that they were commanded to fulfill this mitzvah until the time when the Temple was destroyed a second time. The first was brought by Moses our teacher. The second was brought by Ezra. Seven others were offered until the destruction of the Second Temple. <u>And the tenth will be brought by the king Mashiach</u>; may he speedily be revealed. Amen, so may it be G-d's will."

This belief has become quite common in that the religious Jews believe the time of the Messiah's arrival is close. They will not lock themselves in to saying that only the Messiah can offer the red heifer as a ritual slaughter, but they do maintain that if a qualified red heifer is to arrive, they believe it is a sign heralding the soon return of the Messiah. This belief is very important because if a red heifer does come and is slaughtered, the mindset of the religious Jews will be very eager to receive someone as the Messiah. We will discuss later the reasons for why it seems quite clear that the religious Jews will accept the antichrist as their Messiah. We know him to be a false deceiver, but their eagerness to build the Third Temple will blind them (John 5:43).

In this chapter I wanted to provide some ancient sources in addition to the Biblical text as to the why and how the religious Jews believe a red heifer slaughter should come about. As Christians, our

---

[6] Jacob Neusner, *The Mishnah : A New Translation* (New Haven, CT: Yale University Press, 1988), 1016.

sole authority is the Biblical text, but we must recognize that the religious Jews are quite adamant in including the traditional sources as authoritative in helping them decide which elements are required concerning the red heifer slaughter ceremony. The fact that it looks like many of their traditions are being fulfilled is also going to convince them that God is on their side in their desire to slaughter the red heifer, rebuild the Third Temple, embrace the antichrist as Messiah, and seek to reinstate the Law of Moses.

I will address more of this belief in a later chapter, but we must remember that the religious Jews reembracing the Law of Moses is not righteous. It is blasphemy and an outright apostasy against God and the work of His Son Jesus the Messiah. If they truly were following Moses as they claimed, they would embrace Jesus. *"Do not think that I will accuse you to the Father. There is one who accuses you: Moses, on whom you have set your hope. For if you believed Moses, you would believe me; for he wrote of me. But if you do not believe his writings, how will you believe my words?"* (John 5:45-47). See also the book of Hebrews, which argues for the supremacy of Jesus over the Temple rituals, and that these rituals served their God given purpose until Jesus arrived. Now that He has was offered as the final sacrifice, their efforts to restore the Mosaic system are no longer honorable to God.

Even though the Biblical text has not changed, and the Mishnah and Talmuds have been locked in for over 1000 years, the current era is showing some modifications in some of the traditional viewpoints. As we saw in this chapter, there oftentimes were multiple opinions on a single topic. What this means is that the various rabbinic groups have the ability to reorient their "conclusion" by revisiting one of the divergent opinions as found in their traditions. In the next chapter, we will address some of the ways in which the current atmosphere in modern Israel is changing – including among the rabbis and within the government of Israel itself.

Chapter 4: The Rabbis are Changing Their Thinking in Recent Years

I cannot say it enough that we are living in exciting times! All the perspectives that have been taught by prophecy teachers for the last 150+ years are now approaching maturity in our current time frame. I have been watching prophecy for 30 years, and I shouldn't say that I am shocked at how fast prophetic developments are accelerating in the present time - but I am! I know I shouldn't be, but I guess shocked is not the best word. Instead, it is thrilling to see all these signs and events begin to converge. I always believed them to be true, but to actually see them happen in my time and in ways that are often surprising is exhilarating. It just brings me back to the theological viewpoints before 1948. So many godly theologians just couldn't believe that Israel would ever become a nation. Some of them even admitted that the Biblical text said they would. Instead of interpreting these in a straightforward literal way, their human thinking looked at the current events of their own day and they changed their interpretation to conform to their current situation. This is folly, and we should not repeat this error.

It is true that we do not have all the information as to how exactly these events will play out. At the same time, what is amazing for us is that we are beginning to see them mature every week. It is no longer speculation or conjecture, it is happening. This should give us prophecy watchers even more reason to lean into the Lord, stay faithful, evangelize and be ready for the Lord's return!

There are two items that have changed recently that contribute to the understanding of not only the Third Temple construction, but also the red heifer slaughter. The first has to do with the change in how the religious Jews view their own presence on the Temple Mount. The second is how quickly the politics in Israel can change and affect prophetic developments.

Let's examine the first item which has changed relatively quickly in the last 30 years, concerning how the rabbis viewed the Temple Mount. As I discussed in the Introduction, after the Jewish army secured the Temple Mount for Israel in the Six Day War, there was a short time of rejoicing that Jerusalem had finally been reunited. That initial rejoicing was followed by a long status quo period where the religious rabbis ruled that Jews were forbidden to enter on to the Temple Mount for fear of contributing to the desecration and uncleanness of the Temple Mount area where the holy temple once stood. This ruling was determined in the absence of a red heifer slaughter or the potential discovery of an ancient cache of red heifer ashes from the 1st century. Since neither of these have occurred and as a result, the rabbis have shown even more concern for the contamination of the Temple Mount. This is the reason why you see most religious Jews praying at the western wall (called the Kotel in Hebrew). Most refuse to go up on the Temple Mount, but instead seek to pray outside the complex or along the western wall tunnels which get you closer to what is believed to be the location of the Holy of Holies of Herod's temple. They need the red heifer ashes to be cleansed and then they would qualify to ascend to the area of the ancient temple without fear of desecrating it according to the traditional consensus viewpoint.

There is an excellent overview of the recent changes in perspectives of many rabbis about the status quo presence of Jews on the Temple Mount at Wikipedia and the *972mag.com* website. The latter contains a March, 2023 article written by Nate Orbach entitled, "The Temple Mount Movement Braces for its Moment." You can search their site for this article. The following is an insightful quote from this article.

> "Finally, under the post-1967 status quo, Jews were permitted entry to the Temple Mount only under tightly controlled conditions that included an express prohibition on prayer and ritual objects, and highly restricted hours of entry and points of access. This status quo was enforced by the Waqf, the Muslim religious authority that oversees the site; the Israeli police; and Muslim volunteers from two groups, the Murabitun (for men) and the Murabitat (for women), who would shout at and

disrupt Jewish visitors, regarding their attempts to pray as a violation of the status quo and an infringement on an Islamic holy site.

Taken together, these obstacles kept the Temple Mount out of the minds of most Jews. Though multiple Temple Mount groups were founded in the years after 1967, they failed to gain much traction: the site remained, for most Israelis, irrelevant, dangerous, and forbidden.

By the 1990s, however, as the Oslo Accords took shape, rabbinical unanimity on the prohibition on Jews ascending to the compound began to crack, and the Temple Mount movement kicked into gear. Though the Oslo process deferred final status negotiations on Jerusalem until later stages, both Israel and the future Palestinian state were expected to claim the city as their capital, potentially sharing sovereignty in the Old City (or even handing over control to an international body, like the UN).

The prospect of giving up further land for peace — which had previously set off drastic rebellions among religious Jewish settlers during earlier peace talks, including a plot to blow up the Temple Mount in the early 1980s by the Jewish Underground terrorist group — provoked a sense of crisis for the expansionist wing of the religious-Zionist movement, and they understood this as their moment to stave off the Oslo catastrophe.

Religious-Zionist leaders in West Bank and Gaza settlements formed the Council of Yesha Rabbis and, after initially calling on Jews to ascend to the Temple Mount, contravening centuries of halachic rulings, announced that visiting the site was not only permissible but should be encouraged by rabbinic authorities."

As you can see, there are fascinating developments among religious Jews in the present time. This is not an accident. Just 30 years ago, it was pretty standard to have a consensus about religious Jews feeling compelled by the rabbinic ban to not go up on the Temple Mount. According to an article in June 2022 by Judah Ari Gross on the Times of Israel website, "The first crack in the consensus on the ban came in 1996, when the rabbinical council of the West Bank published a ruling that deemed it permissible to go up to the Temple Mount and encouraged rabbis who agreed with this view to do so with their congregants. In 2000, one of the co-founders of the Temple Institute, Rabbi Yisrael Ariel, released his own ruling that went further, arguing that visiting the Temple Mount was necessary to fulfill the biblical commandment of conquering the land of Israel, which meant that ascending the mount was not only permissible but required under Jewish law."

Now, there are various groups competing for the hearts and minds of the religious Jews in encouraging them to break the historic rabbinic consensus and ascend on to the Temple Mount complex itself. In 2022, there were close to 50,000 religious Jews going up, and this year it is already on pace to exceed that number. There is a fervor building in the ethos of these modern movements. They believe and feel that the arrival of the Messiah is coming soon. We agree, but we also know that their view of the Messiah is far different than the true Biblical view knowing that Jesus is the fulfillment.

Today, there are three major groups who are increasing the pressure and public outcry to have equal access to the Temple Mount for Jews. They are still not allowed to go up and pray, which clearly is discriminatory. You can learn more about the various movements at templeinstitute.org, templemountfaithful.org and thirdtemple.org.

The history of the majority of religious Jews and their rabbis being against going up on the Temple Mount is changing. This has been becoming more apparent ever since the 1990s, and now we see an overwhelming resistance to the rabbinic prohibitions for Jews to ascend on the Temple Mount complex. In fact, many religious Jews are encouraging other religious Jews to simply ignore the rabbinic prohibitions. This is the first time in my 30 years of watching prophecy that this level of religious fervor for the Temple Mount is becoming mainstream.

The second and biggest challenge ever since the 1967 takeover of eastern Jerusalem and the Temple Mount is the political situation. In my introduction chapter, I wrote how only 7 days after the Six Day War ended, Moshe Dayan gave back religious control to the WAQF. Since the beginning of the modern state of Israel, the largest political parties have been relatively irreligious and socialistic. This means that even though many religious groups have tried to create changes of the status quo for the Temple Mount, the government of Israel has been the main impediment. From a practical and political standpoint this has made good sense. The majority of the politicians are secular or simply culturally Jewish. They don't feel the same level of commitment or the need to have a temple rebuilt and have sought to reduce tension with the Muslims over Temple Mount claims. This position has maintained relative peace and harmony through the decades. Most secular politicians did not feel it was worth it to upset the status quo.

This attitude has changed dramatically from around 2010 to the current political make up. The Israeli Knesset (parliament) is made up of 120 seats. It is a multi-party system which is quite different than the American system. In the Israeli system, the majority (61 seats) makes the decision for whom will be Prime Minister. However, no single party has ever won more than 56 seats. This means that a coalition of different parties must unite together to represent more than the 61 seats required to appoint a Prime Minister from one of the coalition groups.

In the past, the religious groups were always in the minority and often ignored. They could be ignored because the secular parties had enough in their coalition to make up the majority. Netanyahu has been the longest serving Prime Minister in Israeli history. He served one term from 1996-1999 by creating a coalition with centrist and religious parties. His second term (2009-2013) consisted of a mixed group of secular and religious groups. His third term (2013-2015) was also a mixed group. Netanyahu's fourth term (2015-2020) was again a mixed group of secularists and religious. This government dissolved and from May 2020 to June 2021, Netanyahu shared a government with Benny Gantz (a secular centrist). This was followed by the Naftali/Lapid government from June 2021 to November 2022. This government was more centrist and secular. The many elections in these years brought significant turmoil and frustration for the average Israeli voter. In November 2022, Netanyahu was able to form a government and this time the only way he was able to form a government was to join with the mostly religious parties. In December 2022, the government that was officially formed is recognized as the most religious government ever in the history of Israeli politics.

    This new government has brought significant changes to the political landscape of Israel. Netanyahu is leading a group of 64 majority seats. This also means that the only way he was able to regain power was to cater to many of the demands of these religious parties. For the first time in the history of Israel, the religious and orthodox parties have the greatest influence ever in the government direction related to the Temple Mount, settlements, relations with the Palestinians, but most specifically, the idea of building a Third Temple.

    Before discussing the potential change to the status quo of the Temple Mount, there was an article written recently which discussed the ways in which the judicial system of Israel could change. This is more evidence of how the new religious government could bring significant changes to theIsraeli court system.

    Currently, Israel has a typical secular judiciary similar to what any democracy might have (the civil courts). However, they allow sanctioned rabbinical courts to have full authority over marriages and divorce when both people are Jewish. For two Jewish people, there are no civil marriages. In addition, the rabbinical courts have authority to determine the authenticity of conversions. This has caused serious issues for Jews or Israelis who become followers of Jesus.

An article from January 2023 entitled, "Torah First: The Judicial Revolution No One is Talking About" comments, "Israeli headlines have been dominated by the proposed legal reform of Justice Minister Yariv Levin, but below the radar, buried deep in the coalition agreements, Likud has agreed with its partners to enact an equally dramatic revolution, which would split the Israeli judicial system and grant rabbinical courts the same powers as any other court. 'You don't need to be an expert to recognize that there's more chance now of the legislation being passed.'" This article and the potential ramifications can be found on the Shomrim.news website. I am not offering an opinion on whether this is a good or bad thing per se, but we do know that as we get closer to the tribulation period, the religious influence will be of such degree that a Third Temple will be built. This reveals once again that the increased religious fervor and political influence that we are now witnessing is evidence that the tribulation period is inching closer and closer. This also means that the rapture is even closer!

Drawing our attention back to the Temple mount, I read that before the new Israeli government was even officially operating, there were various articles demonstrating how the new very religious government could seek to change the status quo on the Temple Mount and cause conflict with the Palestinian and Jordanian groups. The following article is representative of that great concern. <https://www.timesofisrael.com/fire-on-the-mount-how-the-new-government-might-shift-policy-at-flashpoint-holy-site/>

In January 2023, National Security Minister Itamar Ben Gvir from the Otzma Yehudit Party, and who is a devout religious Jew, ascended to the Temple Mount to challenge the general status quo. He is an ardent religious Jew who has made very public comments that the discrimination against Jewish prayer on the Temple Mount should be stopped and that the Jews should be able to build their own temple on the platform. Back in July 2015, there were some religious Jews who set fire to the Benedictine Church of the Multiplication of the Loaves and Fishes. The church was severely damaged and one of the perpetrators was convicted and sentenced to four years in prison. The defense lawyer for the perpetrators was none other than Itamar Ben Gvir. There has been an increase in assaults and persecutions of Christians living in Israel and many believe that Itamar Ben Gvir has not done enough as Security Minister to hold those criminals accountable for their actions.

Along this line of thinking, there is growing concern with the increased ultra-orthodox element in the Israeli government that there will be amplified hostility towards evangelical Christians. Joel Rosenberg recently wrote a public appeal to Prime Minister Benjamin Netanyahu. In an AllIsrael.com article, Joel writes, "Specifically, the Ministry of Interior — currently led by Minister Moshe Arbel, an ultra-Orthodox rabbi and Knesset Member who is part of the religious Shas political party — has stopped issuing clergy visas for staff working at the International Christian Embassy Jerusalem (ICEJ) and similar Christian Zionist groups" (August 18, 2023). Will this continue? We cannot be sure, but what is sure is that the new government is outspoken about bringing changes to Israeli society. Benjamin Netanyahu understands and appreciates the value of the evangelical Christian community support for the nation of Israel. So far, it does not seem that some in the ultra-orthodox factions in the government share Netanyahu's perspective.

Another example of how this current government is becoming much more public in their advocating for a change in the status quo on the Temple Mount happened in June 2023. Knesset member Amit Halevi (of the Likud party) proposed a plan where the Temple Mount authority would be shared. The Muslims would control the southern end of the 37-acre site and the Jews would gain control of the central and northern area. These sorts of pronouncements will only likely increase under this new government. Itamar Ben Gvir once again visited the Temple Mount during the Tish B'Av annual fast day (July 27, 2023). This fast day remembers that the destruction of both Jewish temples happened on the 9th day of the month of Av. Two other Knesset members joined Gvir on the Temple Mount visit and called for increased control. They were quoted as calling it the "the holy place of the people of Israel," and said, "On this day, more than ever – may we be granted complete redemption and the building of the Temple soon in our days, Amen!" These are just a few instances of how the political mood is changing in seeking to remove the discrimination against Jews praying or having access to the Temple Mount.

There is certainly much that could happen in the coming months and years, but the overall attitude is changing. All these events provide more evidence that we are entering into the era of convergence when not only the religious Jews are changing their tune, but the political winds of change are increasing the likelihood that the ritual slaughter of the red heifer and the building of the Third Temple are getting close.

I want to reveal one last amazing piece of information concerning the politics of Israel. I had the opportunity to interview a man named Robert Mawire in December 2022 down near Fort Worth, Texas at his office. Dr. Robert Mawire is well known in Israel for his philanthropic efforts and for helping to modernize the city of Ariel, Israel. He was given an award by the state of Israel for his contributions to the advancement of Israel society. You can see a bio here: https://israelallies.org/dr-robert-mawire. He has had several interactions with Prime Minister Benjamin Netanyahu over the last 20 years. They are on a first name basis.

During my interview, Dr. Mawire shared that in his last conversation with Netanyahu, the Prime Minister told Mawire that after much prayer, he personally felt that it was his destiny as a leader of Israel to be the Prime Minister who finally sees the Third Temple rebuilt. I was not there to hear this myself, but Dr. Mawire gave me permission to share this information and declared its authenticity as he heard it personally. Could this be another example of how God is shaping the political mindset in Israel in order to see the Third Temple rebuilt so that the end time scenario of the return of Jesus can be accomplished? We can only wait and see as we watch all the various elements mentioned in this chapter coming to fruition.

In fact, the red heifer slaughter and the actual construction of the Third Temple are the last remaining items to be put into place before full blown sacrifices can be reinstated in Jerusalem.

In the next chapter, we will explore some of the other preparations that have already been completed and are just waiting for a temple to be rebuilt. All of these preparations are great conversation starters and are a sure way to show that prophecy is being fulfilled in the present time. I believe God has allowed these items well in advance so that we can make the most of every opportunity to share with people that the end of the age has arrived. We should encourage others that we must be ready to meet the Lord Jesus at the rapture at any time!

Chapter 5: The Pre-Temple Preparations

Because the Jewish leadership rejected Jesus as Messiah in the first century, Jesus predicted that judgment would come upon that generation (Matthew 11:16; 12:39, 41, 42, 45). In addition, when Jesus entered Jerusalem on Palm Sunday, instead of rejoicing over Jerusalem, He wept over it. He predicted that Jerusalem and many of the people in it would be destroyed because they did not recognize Him (Luke 19:41-45; 21:20-25). We know that in AD 70, Jesus's words came true, and many Jews were exiled or killed. Another revolt took place in AD 132-135 under a man named Bar Kokhba, and after Rome defeated him, they expelled all Jews from the city of Jerusalem under pain of death and renamed the city Aelia Capitolina.

Since those times, religious Jewish people everywhere have three times per day prayed what is known as the Amidah prayer. This invocation consists of 19 blessings, and two of them refer to the regathering of Israel and the restoration of Jerusalem. Many of the various groups also add an addendum to this prayer specifically asking for the Third Temple to be rebuilt. This is also seen historically at the end of the Passover seder where it is said, "Next year in (rebuilt) Jerusalem." The longing for a restored Jerusalem with the Third Temple as its central focus has been in the hearts and minds of religious Jews since the 1st century AD destruction of the Second Temple.

It is quite comforting to know that God is the sovereign Lord of history. He is providentially working His prophetic plan, regardless of the schemes of wicked mankind. This also includes the desire of His covenant people to build the Third Temple. As we saw in the Introduction, God predicted that a Third Temple would be rebuilt, but only according to His perfect timing. This timing is the end of the age before His Son Jesus returns to set up His eternal kingdom. As I will show, all other attempts were thwarted providentially by God because it was not the proper prophetic time.

The first effort to try and rebuild the temple was under the new Roman Emperor Hadrian (AD 117-138). The Jewish Encyclopedia online has a helpful entry on the Bar Kokhba revolt and they provide other ancient sources for reference. In that article they write that Hadrian initially granted the Jewish people permission to rebuild the temple. After beginning the preparations, a slanderous report by the Samaritans to Hadrian caused him to stop the forward movement of reconstructing the temple. This eventually led to the Bar Kokhba revolt (AD 132-135) which was crushed, and the building of the temple being interrupted.

The second attempt was very short lived and instigated by the Roman Emperor known colloquially as Julian the Apostate (AD 361-363). Julian was the nephew of Constantine the Great and at the age of 20 abandoned his Christian upbringing with the goal of reintroducing paganism to the Roman Empire. Part of this process was encouraging the Jews living in the land of Israel to rebuild and restore their temple with sacrifices. He even offered tax exemptions and other incentives to finish the temple. Some Jews were eager to accept these offers, but factions between the priestly lines and the rabbis created an overall ambivalence to accepting help from a pagan ruler. Additionally, some sources say there were miraculous fires and earthquakes which prevented the work from continuing unabated. Julian died within two years of his ascendancy to the emperor position and the dreams of a rebuilt temple once again faded into dormancy.

The third short-lived attempt occurred early in the 7th century under the Iranian Empire known as the Sassanid. Their military conquered the land of Israel and removed the Christian rulership. In the absence of the western Byzantine (Christian) governance, the Jews seized the opportunity and attempted to restart sacrifices. This did not materialize into anything permanent as the Muslims entered the area around AD 630. The fact that the Muslims controlled this area for over 1300 years prevented any substantial and long-term efforts to rebuild a Jewish Jerusalem or a Third Temple. It was not until the recapture of east Jerusalem after the Six-Day War of 1967 that the dream of a future temple would have any realistic hope.

As we learned in the previous chapter, there are three main groups that have been actively seeking and preparing for the Third

Temple. Realizing and hoping after the situation changed on the Temple Mount, the first group to begin its efforts was the Temple Mount Faithful (started in 1967) and was originally led by Gershon Solomon, who died in November 2022. A second and more recent group is the Third Temple Project. It is a consortium of various organizations worldwide who are dedicated to the rebuilding of the Third Temple. It has an excellent website with all the various efforts separated into categories. These include legal, architecture, politics, construction, education and media. It also has an interactive portion on the various sections of the Temple Mount itself. The website: thirdtemple.org is worth checking out.

    The most well-known organization is the Temple Institute founded in 1987 (templeinstitute.org). This group also has an extensive website with stunning pictures of the various preparations they have made for the coming temple. They have by far done the most extensive work in making and preparing every conceivable object needed for a fully functioning sacrificial system. The following is a table of all the various implements that the Temple Institute has fabricated. A great opportunity would be to visit their museum in Jerusalem to see all of these items. They also have pictures of most of these items on their website.

Item	Purpose
Copper laver	For Kohanim to wash at start of day
Mizrak	Holds blood from sacrificial animals
Large mizrak	Holds blood from larger animals
Three-pronged fork	To arrange offerings on the altar
Measuring cup	To measure meal offerings
Copper vessel for meal offerings	To prepare meal offerings
Silver shovel	To remove ashes from the altar

Silver vessel for wine libation	For wine accompanying offerings
Lottery box	For Yom Kippur
Silver altar cup for water libation	For Sukkot
Silver libation vessels	For Sukkot
Sickle	To reap the Omer barley
Other offering implements	To offer the Omer barley
Abuv	To roast the Omer barley
Menorah cleansing vessel	To clean the Menorah
Oil pitcher	For replenishing the Menorah
Small golden flask	For replenishing individual Menorah lamps
Frankincense censer	Used for the incense offering
Incense chalice	For Ketoret or incense offering
Incense shovel	For Ketoret or incense offering
Menorah	See Menorah
Table of the Showbread	See Showbread
Incense altar	For Ketoret or incense offering
Ark of the Covenant (mockup)	See Ark of the Covenant
Crown	Crown worn by the High Priest
Garments of the High Priest	See High Priest
Silver trumpets	Announce special occasions and offerings
Gold-plated shofar	For Rosh Hashanah
Silver-plated shofar	For fast days

Harp	Used by the choir of Levites singing psalms
Lyre	Used by the choir of Levites singing psalms
Crimson Dye	Used in red heifer ceremony

If you visit the Temple Institute YouTube page, you can find three videos under the "Holy Temple Building Plans" playlist where they have animated walk throughs of the coming Third Temple. Over $100,000 was spent on architectural plans and much of what has been designed is found in those animations. They are well worth checking out.

Rabbi Aryeh Lipo has been organizing and preparing stones in advance of the day that official government permission will be granted for the construction of the Third Temple. These stones are cut with tools, but once brought up on to the Temple Mount area, no tools are allowed.

Another interesting aspect to all the various utensils and vessels in the table presented on the previous pages is the ways in which others are becoming involved in the various musical preparations for the anticipated worship services. Ariel Louis, who lives in Israel, is making hand-crafted Baroque flutes from wood that is at least 80 years old. Adam Berkowitz wrote a fascinating article on Israel365news.com with the title, "Creating handmade wooden flutes for the Third Temple." Ariel Louis's late father, Rabbi David Louis, was commissioned by the Temple Institute to compose specific music for future celebrations. You can also read about these preparations at the same site written by Adam Berkowitz with the title, "What is the Last Secret to Be Revealed Before the Messiah?"

In addition to the priestly garments that have been meticulously crafted, priests (kohanim) are being trained to perform their services in a completed temple. Their school is called Kehuna Academy and can be found online providing free classes and seeks to unite any and all who qualify as priests to become equipped. Rivkah

Lambert Adler wrote an article which can be searched and found online entitled, "When The Third Temple Is Built, These Temple Priests Will Be Ready To Serve." She does a full report of the various priests who have been in training and will be ready when the time comes.

One of the ceremonial aspects of the red heifer ritual slaughter involves children. The children were put on animals and led to the pool of Siloam in ancient times where they would let down buckets to retrieve the fresh living spring water from the pool which arrives from the Gihon spring. They would ride the animals and take this water up to the Mount of Olives where it would be mixed with the ashes of the red heifer. Today, there is a group of children who were born in a complex which is only built on bedrock. As we discussed before, bedrock is the sure way of knowing that you are not walking on any sort of grave which would bring contamination. So, these children have been born and raised in a situation where they have always been on bedrock and thus are guaranteed to be ritually clean. They will be involved in the future red heifer ceremony. This is just one more layer of preparation which is being fulfilled in our generation.

It is becoming difficult to keep up with all the various actions and training of the various priests in preparation for the coming temple. In October 2022, over 600 Levites joined together in a worship service rehearsal on the southern steps of the Temple Mount. Also in recent times, water libations and Shavuot grain offering ceremonies have been performed near the Temple Mount. These liturgical rehearsals were unheard of at this level before 1967. According to rabbi Yitzhak Momo in a report from CBN, the Temple Institute currently has 9 pure priests. What this means is that they have not traveled to places where they could become contaminated from graves or touching a dead person. We are truly living in exciting times as all these events are pointing to the Lord Jesus's soon return for the catching away of His church!

One final event worth mentioning happened in August 2019 and also was reported by Adam Berkowitz from the

Israel365news.com site. Professor Zohar Amar, a Professor in the Department of Land of Israel Studies at Bar-Ilan University, has long been interested in taking a scientific approach to the Biblical text. For the first time in modern history (and maybe longer), someone in the land of Israel decided to perform a practice test of the burning of a cow with the intention of following the stipulations as outlined in the Bible and rabbinical writings.

Professor Amar kept exact records of the amount of wood used in the ritual slaughter along with how many kilograms of ash was left after burning the 270-kilogram (594 lbs.) cow and the wood. It was reported that he did not use a red heifer, but instead a sick adult cow.

Before starting the fire, a rectangular pit was carved into the bedrock. The pit was around 14 feet long, 6.5 feet wide and 3 feet deep. Inside this trough, a pyre of pine and oak wood were combined for the fuel. The cow was slaughtered first, and then lifted up onto the pyre of wood. Once ignited, the fire reached a whopping 940 degrees in just over two hours. To burn the cow and all the wood took nine hours. It then took a few days for the ashes to cool down enough to collect and measure. The total remaining amount of ash including 11 kilograms (24 lbs.) from the animal itself ended up being 145 lbs. of ash.

According to the requirements, this ash was then mixed with spring water. The final conclusion was that each gram of ash could be added to 1000 liters of water. From the yield of 145 lbs. of ash, this experiment proved to be enough for 660 billion sprinklings! What this ultimately means is that even though there are several current red heifer candidates at the moment, one cow would be enough for many generations of sprinkling. This amount would also be sufficient for the cleansing of the entire Temple Mount area in preparation for the construction of the Third Temple.

In the next chapter we will discuss the details of the various efforts and historical searches for a red heifer. It has not been too long, but there were some endeavors that preceded the latest arrival of the five red heifers from a ranch in Texas.

Chapter 6: The Modern Search for the Red Heifer

We learned in a previous chapter that the medieval rabbi Maimonides recorded that there were nine red heifers that were slaughtered from Moses to Ezra and then 7 more up until the Second Temple was destroyed in AD 70. He also stated around AD 1200 that the final 10th red heifer to be slaughtered would herald the Messianic Era. Once Israel became a nation and Jerusalem (including the Temple Mount) was at least superficially in the hands of the Jewish people, there became a greater interest and focus on the not forgotten dream of rebuilding the temple.

The Beginning Searches (1980s-2020)

The study of prophecy in the modern church age took on greater influence with the publication of *The Late Great Planet Earth* by Hal Lindsey in 1970. This book sold over 28 million copies by 1990, and these 20 years of influence had a direct bearing on the red heifer search. As we will see, several evangelical Christian ranchers developed a love for Israel and for seeing prophecy fulfilled. They also were aware that the Jewish people needed or desired to procure a red heifer in order to provide cleansing ashes not only for a future priesthood, but also for the Temple Mount proper where a temple would hopefully be erected.

Rabbi Chaim Richman in his book, *The Mystery of the Red Heifer,* describes his first experience with these evangelical Christians who came to Israel in the spring of 1990 to visit the Temple Institute and gain more firsthand information of what was required for the red heifer to be qualified. One of these individuals was Revered Clyde Lott of Canton Mississippi. It was in the previous year (1989) that Clyde was studying Genesis 30 and began to ponder how he could help develop a specific breed of red cow.

Over the next few years and several trips to Israel, Clyde Lott and Rabbi Richman developed a plan to "help bring about a livestock and agricultural restoration throughout the land of Israel." In the early

1990s, they were able to help establish increased efficiency and knowledge for the cattle industry of Israel. Part of this was to engender ways in which this cattle infrastructure would lend to the focus of breeding red heifers which might one day be used in preparation for the coming temple.

The first real excitement came on November 11, 1994, when Rabbi Chaim Richman traveled to Clyde's Canton, Mississippi ranch to examine 4 red heifers. After an extensive examination, Rabbi Richman declared one of them to be preliminarily qualified as the first red heifer candidate in 2000 years. As has been the case since this first candidate, a red heifer that is qualified can become unqualified by growing more than 2 non-red hairs out of a single follicle, becoming blemished, or other reasons. As cows get older, they often grow out of their younger colors of hair. Eventually, that first red heifer became disqualified.

Even with that initial disappointment, the Temple Institute has not given up in continuing to seek to establish ranches in the land of Israel dedicated to home grow a red heifer. Other groups have joined in the establishment of procedures, processes, and ranches to facilitate the goal of finding a fully qualified red heifer.

My friend Jeff Vanhatten has also been watching the developments for a couple of decades. He has a website called raptureparty.net with a lot of prophetic material. He writes concerning the red heifer search, "The Temple Institute had identified two candidates, one in 1997 and another in 2002, both initially thought to have met the requirements, but later found each to be unsuitable. The headlines read: "Apocalypse Cow" in the New York Times (1997) and "News Flash: Red Heifer Born In Israel" in a Temple Institute web posting (2002). In 2014 the headlines read "Torah-Condition-For-Third-Temple-Now-Met", and articles reported that the Temple Institute had posted a video showing what appeared to be a perfect red heifer that was being raised at an unidentified location in the United States. A report from Right Side News said a "qualified" red heifer has not been seen in Israel for nearly 2,000 years."

"In 2015 the Temple Institute in Jerusalem established a breeding program called "Raise a Red Heifer in Israel" to raise the necessary items needed for purification of the temple and its priests. Israeli law does not allow the importation of live cattle into Israel, so the Temple Institute imported frozen embryos of red Angus cows from the United States and implanted them into the wombs of Israeli domestic cows."

There were a few other potential candidates in 2018 and 2019, which also ended up being disqualified. The fact that all of these previous cows became disqualified has led some people to become skeptical of the entire search process. I often get comments that the red heifer search is being overblown and that nothing will ever come of it because God is against it. Personally, I have no skin in the game and I am not a prophet, so I do not know exactly how it will play out. But what we do know is that the modern rabbinic consensus shows that this search is not going away. In fact, it is increasing as the rabbis have now officially become convinced that the red heifer does not need to be born in Israel. They would prefer that for sure, but their search now is getting the best results from ranches in the USA.

The Latest 5 Red Heifers (Arrived in Israel September 15, 2022)

As we saw earlier, Clyde Lott was the first American rancher that became directly involved with the rabbis in the search for a red heifer. This set the precedent for cooperation between those in Israel and those in the USA. For those watching over the last 30+ years, there was always a nervous optimism because there was usually only one red heifer at a time being examined. This means that if one became a potential candidate, there was much anticipation, but then also disappointment when it became disqualified. Subsequently, it was often years before there was even another singular candidate.

This latest situation has caused a greater level of optimism for many because there are now 5 candidates at once. It is not possible to give the background without introducing the main person behind all this breeding effort, and that is Byron Stinson. He is a part-time rancher, but more of a businessman that lives in Texas, and also lives near Bethlehem during portions of the year. He loves Israel and is a vocal member of the organization called Boneh Israel (see chapter 3 for more info on this organization). He has done many other projects in Israel which can be found on their website. Byron is known as a Gentile who is showing love to the people and land of Israel by sponsoring and actively participating in these various projects.

I interviewed Byron Stinson and our conversation can be found on the Prophecy Watchers YouTube channel by searching for "prophecy watchers red heifer" or you can go to this URL- https://tinyurl.com/red-heifer.

Before going into detail about Byron's participation, it would be good to go back to 1991 and discuss Ty Davenport, who we first learned about in chapter 3. Ty is a cattle rancher who rededicated his life to Jesus in 1991. He had read Numbers 19 and felt that the Lord was revealing to him that one of his purposes in life was to help prophecy be fulfilled and provide a red heifer to Israel. He changed his cattle herds to red angus and his dad helped him out by finding a premier red angus in Montana and bringing it back to his ranch in Texas. While all these efforts were going on behind the scenes, Ty did not yet have the contacts to help fulfill what he perceived as his calling.

In early 2021, rabbis had reached out to Byron Stinson, who had become friends with many of them through his various contacts in Israel and also his work through Boneh Israel. They knew that he was from Texas and had many connections there with ranchers. They asked him to help them find a red heifer. Byron's team began to do some research and got some data of the various ranchers who were focused on red cattle. To improve their chances for success, they mailed out letters, took out magazine ads, and sent text messages to phones. Finally, in June of 2021, they got some responses and began to get some opportunities. Byron mentioned that cows are born usually in the spring and the fall, and since this was June, they would have opportunity to see the spring cattle. Yet there was one problem. Any cows that they might go see in June would have been born a couple of months earlier. This means that those new calves would have received the normal tag in the ear. This tag would blemish the calf, no matter how perfectly red it was. The procedure created a situation where they would have to find a cow that was about to give birth, so that the new calf would not be tagged and blemished.

Through some providential circumstances, a gentleman from Denton, Texas, who was a fan of LA Marzulli, made contact with me in Oklahoma City in September 2022. He had some giant skeletons that he wanted to give to LA, so I invited him to bring them up in October and to meet with LA as he was in town filming with us. We had a great time of fellowship and by happenstance (cf. Ruth 2:3) I mentioned to this gentleman that I was working on a book on the red heifers that had just arrived in Israel on September 15, 2022. He got excited and told me that he was friends with another gentleman named Dr. Robert Mawire who was involved in the transaction and that he would get me connected. I introduced him at the end of chapter 5. His office is near Fort Worth and I was planning on being in Dallas in early December 2022 for the pre-trib.org conference. So, we set up a meeting and I made my way to his office and met with him and a few associates.

Dr. Mawire is a very busy man, and his Mondays are always reserved for meetings and other items of business. Yet he said he felt led by the Lord to make time for our meeting. I am extremely grateful for his graciousness and hospitality. He spent 4 hours with me discussing the details of the red heifers and about his involvement. It was a true honor to gain access to first-hand information about the entire process. Dr. Mawire is well known in Israel and has 35 years of experience working with the Israel government and in the development of the advanced technological city of Ariel, Israel. He mentioned that some rabbis reached out to him soliciting his help to procure some red heifers from Texas. He is quite passionate and energetic in describing how he has learned through the years that he cannot get ahead of the Lord's guidance. So, instead of trying to do it in his own strength, he decided he would pray and wait on the Lord.

The very next day he received a phone call from his friend Brian Davenport (see chapter 3 for his biography). Dr. Mawire did not reveal how Brian even knew to call him, but he took it as a divine answer to prayer. Brian revealed to Dr. Mawire that his brother Ty had been raising red heifers since the 1980s. He arranged a trip to go see Ty the next day. He called Byron Stinson and together they went the next day to go see the new calves which were born October 5-12, 2021.

A few months later in January 2022, two rabbis (Chanan Kupietzky and Tzachi Mamo) visited the ranch in Rockwall, Texas to observe the young red heifers. Chanan had been involved with Byron in other searches around the USA. In March, other rabbis came and did some inspections at the Davenport ranch. In all the searching, there were at least 21 cows found, but when the time came, only five were chosen to be flown to Israel. There are still 16 qualified cows at the ranch in Rockwall, Texas.

Israel has a restriction against importing cows into their country. This caused some challenges to get them into the country and eventually they had to be labeled as pets.

The two different breeds ended up being Saint Gertrudis and Red Angus. These five were driven from Texas to JFK airport destined for an American Airlines 777 airliner. A couple other complications arose. One was that the cows had to be insured for their flight over. Byron told me that this created some challenges and the case was sent to some actuaries in order to determine the cost of insuring the animals. The final cost for insuring the cows… 15 shekels per cow. In today's exchange rates, about $4.03. The second challenge was that the temperature when the cows landed in Tel Aviv had to be less than 88 degrees Fahrenheit. They had to abort the mission twice, but they finally landed in Tel Aviv on September 15, 2022.

The Jerusalem post reported, "The heifers were greeted by a ceremony at Ben-Gurion Airport. Temple Institute officials Rabbi Chanan Kupietzky, Rabbi Tzachi Mamo, Rabbi Yisrael Ariel and Rabbi Azaria Ariel participated in the ceremony, alongside Stinson and Director-General Netanel Isaac of the Jerusalem and Heritage Ministry."

The cows were purchased for $100,000 each, and it cost around $200,000 to fly them to Israel. This is quite the expense for sure, but the Temple Institute and others are serious about seeing the red heifer commandment fulfilled. The cows were taken to a secure and undisclosed location in the north, but that is changing.

I was in Israel in April 2022 and the beginnings of a brand-new visitor's center in Shiloh was taking shape. As of July 2022, the building is up and one of the red heifers has been moved to this site. Eventually another will come and be available to be viewed by the public, but the public will not be able to touch the animals. The remaining three will be kept at a private ranch at an undisclosed location.

As was mentioned prior, the earliest any of the 5 red heifers will be old enough is October or November 2023. That is coming soon, but the expected ceremony is planned to happen at Passover 2024 under tight security.

Byron Stinson told me that permits and permissions from the Israeli government are already under way. With the new religious government, I would be surprised if the answer comes back "No." These are just more evidence of the convergence of the times that we are living in. Chuck Missler used to say, "These are not signs of the times, but more specifically we are living in the times of the signs!" I agree.

In the next chapter we will discuss the theological significance of the red heifer and the ministry of Jesus as found in the New Testament.

Chapter 7: What is the New Testament Significance of the Red Heifer

For the New Testament (NT) or New Covenant Christian, there can be tremendous confusion as to how we connect and understand the Old Testament (OT) and the NT. This chapter is going to be more theological than the rest, but a good foundational understanding is needed. I hope by the end of this chapter that you will understand how God prepared the way in the OT for the coming of Jesus, and how His once and for all sacrifice on the cross was the perfect fulfillment securing for us our salvation. This understanding will also explain why the religious Jews today, who reject Jesus and the NT, are confused.

Paul was a Pharisee and certainly was entrenched in all things Jewish and Hebrew. Paul writes about his own heritage, *"If anyone else thinks he has reason for confidence in the flesh, I have more: circumcised on the eighth day, of the people of Israel, of the tribe of Benjamin, a Hebrew of Hebrews; as to the law, a Pharisee; as to zeal, a persecutor of the church; as to righteousness under the law, blameless. But whatever gain I had, I counted as loss for the sake of Christ. Indeed, I count everything as loss because of the surpassing worth of knowing Christ Jesus my Lord. For his sake I have suffered the loss of all things and count them as rubbish, in order that I may gain Christ and be found in him, <u>not having a righteousness of my own that comes from the law, but that which comes through faith in Christ, the righteousness from God that depends on faith</u>—"* (Philippians 3:4-9). Paul understood not just the OT, but also the Jewish traditions which later became known as the rabbinic traditions. Yet Paul recognized that many of the Jews back then and we see that even today they still seek to attain a righteousness that comes from the law (and sacrifices) and not through faith.

Paul also wrote, *"I am a Jew, born in Tarsus in Cilicia, but brought up in this city, educated at the feet of Gamaliel according to the strict manner of the law of our fathers, being zealous for God as all of you are this day"* (Acts 22:3). Seeking to understand the OT is not simply a matter of a difference of opinion, but it is a matter of salvation. The Bible says clearly that those who reject Jesus and His salvation are not saved. There is no other way to get to the Father except through Jesus (John 14:6; Acts 4:12).

Does this mean that those religious Jews today who pray many times a day, read the OT, and are seeking to slaughter the red heifer and build the Third Temple are unsaved? This is not my opinion or any earthly human's opinion, but Jesus Himself says this is the case in John 14:6.

Paul also writes about those Jews who do not embrace Jesus, *"Brothers, my heart's desire and prayer to God for them is that <u>they may be saved</u>. For I bear them witness that they have a zeal for God, but not according to knowledge. For, being ignorant of the righteousness of God, and seeking to establish their own, they did not submit to God's righteousness. For Messiah (Christ) is the end of the law for righteousness to everyone who believes"* (Romans 10:1-4). Paul says that they are currently lost and not saved, because they seek to establish their own righteousness and did not submit to the righteousness which is imputed to everyone through faith in Jesus the Messiah.

It is not my intention to sound mean or arrogant by saying that religious Jews are confused. Paul writes that they indeed have a zeal for God, but it is not based on New Covenant knowledge (Romans 10:3-4). The reason they remain confused and lost is because they do not embrace Jesus as Messiah. Paul writes: *"But their minds were hardened. For to this day, when they read the old covenant, that same veil remains unlifted, because only through Messiah is it taken away. Yes, to this day whenever Moses is read a veil lies over their hearts. But when one turns to the Lord Jesus, the veil is removed"* (2 Corinthians 3:14-16). Paul loved his fellow Jews and sought to win them to Jesus on every occasion. He loved them and treated them with respect. I will discuss this more in a subsequent chapter. He was heartbroken over their refusal to seek Jesus, and we should be also (Romans 9:1-2).

What then was the purpose of the Mosaic Law and its 613 commandments (including the red heifer commandment)? In short, all of these rituals, ceremonies, and commandments were given as object lessons to increase the faith of the people and to point forward to the time when Jesus would come and fulfill all these shadows. People had always been saved by grace through faith since the beginning of time. (You can find a short paper I wrote on this subject at https://prophecywatchers.com/salvation-in-the-old-testament/).

Paul discussed the value of the all the festivals, rituals, and holy days found under the Mosaic Law. He said, *"And you, who were dead in your trespasses and the uncircumcision of your flesh, God made alive together with him, having forgiven us all our trespasses, by canceling the record of debt that stood against us with its legal demands. This he set aside, nailing it to the cross. He disarmed the rulers and authorities and put them to open shame, by triumphing over them in him. Therefore let no one pass judgment on you in questions of food and drink, or with regard to a festival or a new moon or a Sabbath. <u>These are a shadow of the things to come, but the substance belongs to Messiah (Christ)</u>"* (Colossians 2:13-17). What Paul shows us is that all of these rituals are simply shadows. This means that they are not the real thing, but instead a shadow of that which was to come, which we know is Jesus and His work on the cross. This is true also of the red heifer slaughter as found in Numbers 19.

When we come to the NT, this truth is not lost on the writer of the book of Hebrews. It is well-known that the author is fully competent in OT Biblical theology. The goal of the book is to seek to convince a group of Jews, who had made a profession of faith in Jesus, not to retreat back into Judaism. They were being persecuted and were contemplating forsaking their outward association with other New Covenant believers (Hebrews 10:34, 25).

The writer seeks to show that Jesus is superior and better than the three main pillars found in Judaism – the revelation from God that came through <u>angels</u>, <u>Moses</u>, and the <u>Levitical priesthood</u>. It is written that the Old Covenant Law and understanding of the entire sacrificial system was given through angels in some capacity that we do not fully know (Galatians 3:19; Acts 7:53). This imparting gives the Law a tremendous level of authority, as does the fact that it was given through the prophet Moses. Today for the Jew (just as back in Jesus's day), there is no greater prophet than Moses, who spoke with God face to face (Exodus 33:11; Numbers 12:8 Deuteronomy 34:10). Since Moses commanded that Aaron become the high priest and institute the entire Levitical system, these sacrificial ceremonies and rituals became the main focus of all Israelite worship after Moses. These practices began in the tabernacle and were followed into the Temple of Solomon and the Second Temple of Jesus's day.

Jesus came on the scene preaching a gospel of repentance (Matthew 4:17; Mark 1:14-15) and for the purpose of offering up His life to fulfill all the requirements of the Law (Matthew 3:15; 5:17). His death would be in fulfillment of Isaiah 53, where His life was given as a substitute for the people, and all who trusted in Him would be saved and find refuge (Psalm 2:12; Luke 24:44-48).

Many years ago, I had been attending a church where a Jewish woman began to visit. After a period of time, it was quite clear that she did not trust the Bible as being true. She said to me that she did not believe in a "slaughterhouse religion" and that the idea of the blood of Jesus was not necessary. I told her I was shocked that she, as a Jewish person, could say such a thing. God instituted this "slaughterhouse religion" as centered in the tabernacle and Temple precincts with an altar, on which thousands (or millions?) of animals were slaughtered over a period of 1500+ years (1446 BC to AD 70). I reminded her that there is a consistency between Leviticus 17:11 which reads, *"For the life of the flesh is in the blood, and I have given it for you on the altar to make atonement for your souls, for it is the blood that makes atonement by the life"* and something similar in Hebrews 9:22 which reads, *"Without the shedding of blood there is no forgiveness of sins."*

The book of Hebrews begins, *"Long ago, at many times and in many ways, God spoke to our fathers by the prophets, but in these last days he has spoken to us by his Son, whom he appointed the heir of all things, through whom also he created the world"* (Hebrews 1:1-2). The book of Hebrews then proceeds to show that Jesus, as the Son of God, is superior to angels (Hebrews 1-2). After showing that the authority of Jesus was better than angels, the book then focuses on the 2nd pillar of authority, namely Moses.

"For Jesus has been counted worthy of more glory than Moses-- as much more glory as the builder of a house has more honor than the house itself. (For every house is built by someone, but the builder of all things is God.) Now Moses was faithful in all God's house as a servant, to testify to the things that were to be spoken later, but Christ is faithful over God's house as a son. And we are his house, if indeed we hold fast our confidence and our boasting in our hope" (Hebrews 3:3-6).

This recognition has to be tough for a Jewish person – not only back in Jesus's day, but also today. Moses is the primary prophet that a modern Jewish person ever looks to as a final authority. Yet Jesus is far superior, and Jesus said that Moses wrote about Him (John 5:46).

Our discussion finally brings us to the third authority, which also has modern application as we discuss the red heifer and the authority of the Levitical priesthood with its sacrifices. We might wonder today why the religious Jews are so fixated on the need to rebuild the Temple in order to start the sacrifices again. This need has been their focus for the last 1950+ years since they rejected Jesus and the Second Temple was destroyed in AD 70. We must also remember that church history has been quite shameful considering the ways in which many so-called Christians treated Jewish people. These Christians slandered, persecuted, and often participated in the killing of Jewish people. This horrendous treatment was quite evident in the various expulsions, pogroms, and crusades. In fact, most Jewish people consider Hitler to be a Christian. Because of the history of the church, it is regrettable that so many Jews today would never consider following Jesus because of the actions of those who have claimed to follow Him.

Granted, the inexcusable actions by some so-called Christians does not excuse the rejection of Jesus by the Jews, but it should elicit in us a sense of compassion, understanding, and humility when addressing this issue by speaking the truth in love (Ephesians 4:15).

The writer of Hebrews shows that Jesus is better than angels and Moses, but how is Jesus better than the Levitical priesthood? The first approach the writer takes is to show that Jesus is also a high priest (Hebrews 4-7), but His priesthood was through a priesthood that is superior, because it preceded the Levitical priesthood. The priesthood of Jesus was according to the superior order of Melchizedek, who was greater than Abraham (Hebrews 7:1-10). So, Jesus has a better priesthood than Levi, and now the writer turns to the fact that even the very sacrifices of Levi were inferior to the once and for all sacrifice of Jesus.

We again see the concept that the OT sacrifices were a shadow pointing to something greater and more permanent. *"For since the law has but a <u>shadow</u> of the good things to come instead of the true form of these realities, it can never, by the same sacrifices that are continually offered every year, make perfect those who draw near. Otherwise, would they not have ceased to be offered, since the worshipers, having once been cleansed, would no longer have any consciousness of sins? But in these sacrifices there is a reminder of sins every year. For it is impossible for the blood of bulls and goats to take away sins"* (Hebrews 10:1-4).

One of my favorite verses in the Bible is found in this chapter, and it is a summary of how the sacrifice of Jesus succeeds where all the OT sacrifices did not. Hebrews 10:14 reads, *"For by one offering He has perfected forever those who are being sanctified."* WOW! Our salvation is extremely secure because of the ONE offering of Jesus, never needing to be repeated again.

In the previous chapter (Hebrews 9), the writer focuses specifically on the day of atonement sacrifice (Leviticus 16) and also the spiritual application of the red heifer slaughter as found in Numbers 19. He writes, *"For if the blood of goats and bulls, and the sprinkling of defiled persons with the ashes of a heifer, sanctify for the purification of the flesh, how much more will the blood of Christ, who through the eternal Spirit offered Himself without blemish to God, purify our conscience from dead works to serve the living God. Therefore, He is the mediator of a new covenant, so that those who are called may receive the promised eternal inheritance, since a death has occurred that redeems them from the transgressions committed under the first covenant"* (Hebrews 9:13-15). As we saw in chapter 2, the red heifer offering was given to provide ashes that would be mixed with water in order to purify someone who outwardly became ritually unclean. The unblemished and burned red heifer's ashes were a shadow which points to the offering of Jesus. The writer to the Hebrews says that the blood of Jesus is not limited to simply purifying the externals, but instead our very conscience! Jesus also is said to be unblemished (Hebrews 4:15) and His offering is far superior to the red heifer.

We know that the red heifer must be slaughtered and burned outside the camp (Numbers 19:3). The author of Hebrews also brings up this requirement as a testimony to the connection that Jesus is the fulfillment of the red heifer slaughter. He writes, *"For the bodies of those animals whose blood is brought into the holy places by the high priest as a sacrifice for sin are burned outside the camp. So, <u>Jesus also suffered outside the gate</u> in order to sanctify the people through His own blood. Therefore, let us go to Him outside the camp and bear the reproach He endured"* (Hebrews 13:11-13).

What then do we say about what the religious Jews are trying to do in reinstituting the slaughter of the red heifer in our modern day? As New Covenant believers, we know that these efforts are fruitless. They cannot and will not ever bring about true purification. This can only happen through the completed and sufficient work of Jesus the Messiah for all people - but for the Jews first (Romans 1:16-17).

However, what it does reveal is that God has a plan to save the Jewish people. Paul tells us that when the time arrives, all the remaining Jewish people will be saved (Romans 11:25-26) through faith in Jesus as Messiah (see Zechariah 12:10). We know that this event is going to happen at the end of the tribulation period. In the meantime, God is allowing them to seek these fruitless efforts of the red heifer and the rebuilding of the Third Temple in order for them to come to understand how spiritually lost they really are. The antichrist will deceive them into a covenant which allows them to sacrifice in the Third Temple, but will then betray them in the middle of the 70th week and cease their sacrifices (Daniel 9:27). He will then go after them to commit full genocide, but God will protect them for another

3.5 years until they come to the place of repentance when Jesus will rescue them at the end of the 7-year tribulation (Rev 12:13-16; Matthew 23:37-39; Hosea 5:15).

What should our attitude be toward the red heifer movement and the rebuilding of the Third Temple? As you might imagine, there are many different viewpoints. I reached out and asked the thoughts from many of your favorite Bible teachers - which I will share with you in the next chapter.

Chapter 8: Your Favorite Prophecy Teachers Respond to the Red Heifer Movement

    As we have seen in previous chapters, there have been many Bible-believing Christians who love Jesus and who have also participated in the movement to rebuild the Third Temple and/or have contributed to finding and supplying the red heifers. This seeming contradiction brings up many questions for the average Christian. As we learned in the previous chapter, we know that the sacrifices in the OT and any new ones that may be implemented will not provide salvation nor effectual forgiveness. That can only come through faith in the finished work of Jesus. Under the OT, the people had faith that their sacrifices were honoring to God, and they were - as long as they were mixed with faith. God received their faith and accounted righteousness to them, as He did with Abraham (Genesis 15:3). We know that God accepted these sacrifices because they pointed forward to the full and sufficient sacrifice of Jesus.

    Since we know the limitations of the sacrificial system (Hebrews 10), we also know that the coming Third Temple, which is prophesied to be built, cannot and will not be honorable to God because it is not mixed with faith in Jesus. Although I will address this topic more in the next chapter, there are three related questions that you may likely be asking yourself:

1) Should Christians be excited about all the preparations for the coming Third Temple and red heifer ritual slaughter?

2) Do you think God would approve of New Covenant Christians who are followers of Jesus to financially contribute to the building of the Third Temple and the acquisition of a red heifer for Israel to ritually slaughter?

3) Would God providentially (or miraculously) provide circumstances (politically, etc.) and materials for the rebuilding of

the Third Temple and red heifer ritual slaughter without officially endorsing it?

I thought you might enjoy the benefit of knowing the thoughts concerning these questions from many of today's most prominent prophecy teachers, and so I asked them to share their wisdom with you. Below are their responses, listed in alphabetical order according to their last name.

Lee Brainard (Soothkeep.info)

1) Should Christians be excited about the preparations for the temple and the red heifer slaughter?

Yes. The preparations of the orthodox for building and operating the temple, including the slaughter of the red heifer, are obviously stage-setting for the events of the seventieth week. It is hard to miss the connection between man's current efforts and God's plans for the temple in the 70th week. The fact that the orthodox are unbelieving is irrelevant. Just as the restoration of Israel to nation status came about through unbelieving men, Jews and Gentiles alike, who were often more political than spiritual in their focus, so the preparations for the temple are going forward through the hands of men who are unsaved. This is the sovereignty and providence of God in the background like we see in the book of Esther. The king's heart is in the Lord's hands.

But the question demands a follow-up question something along the lines of, "In what way and degree?" I have seen a slew of material on social media with teachers hyperventilating about the red heifers and the nearness of the rapture. The rapture will be this fall or next year at the latest! The temple is going to be built next year! We won't be here next year! This is sensationalism at its finest. A healthy focus on the subject would regard the red heifers as one cog in the machinery of the temple preparations, and it would regard the temple-preparations as one aspect of the prophetic convergence that is setting the stage for events that are going to happen after the church meets the Lord in the clouds. There is nothing in the temple preparations themselves or in the five red heifers from Texas that puts us on red alert for the nearness of the rapture and the rebuilding of the temple. Nothing says this fall or next year. Nothing demands in the next couple years.

One thing that needs to be understood is that there is no guarantee that any of the five will prove to be unblemished come their final test. Ditto for the red heifers being raised at several other locations in the Golan. I have been watching the red heifer story since the 80s when the focus was on finding the existing ashes. In the 90s the focus shifted to raising red heifers. Over and over again, speculation on red heifer candidates went into overdrive. The result was always the same. The over-hyped information nosedived. The only thing that is certain when it comes to the current temple and red heifer developments is that the temple movement is dead serious about rebuilding the temple and vetting an unblemished red heifer and burning it for its ashes. This earnestness is a subset of the fig-tree-generation prophecy---a significant development within the flow of events which began with the physical resurrection of the nation of Israel. In ancient Israel the temple and politics are closely intertwined. So it is now. There will be no rebuilding of the temple unless and until the current political climate changes. Ultimately, the tribulation temple will be sandwiched between the two main political figureheads of the last days: the antichrist and the true Messiah. The false messiah will permit the rebuilding of the temple. God will own this temple as his temple. The antichrist will sit in it, declare himself God, and erect an image in it, the whole effort being the abomination of desolation. Then the Lord will come to his temple.

Assuming that at least one of the five red heifers will remain unblemished, we have two years until their final examination if the Temple Institute follows the traditional rabbinical interpretation of the ancient sages and Rabbi Meir as taught in Mishna Parah 1:1. If they follow the minority position of Rabbi Eliezer (also mentioned in Mishna Parah 1:1), we have a wait of a year. The latter does seem to be their inclination (see their FB post from Sept 19, 2022 entitled, "More About Our 5 Red Heifer Candidates). Time will tell which of the two views prevails. But assuming that they test, sacrifice, and burn the red heifer in one year or two, they will still be at a political standstill for rebuilding the temple. The ashes will have to be stored, and the temple faithful will have to wait. In the current political climate, there seems to be no possibility of the temple being built. Something big has to happen to change the status quo. Judging by history, we could be waiting for decades to see the temple rebuilt. This won't be case. Most likely the big events that prepare the way will be the destruction of Israel's immediate enemies (Ps. 83), the destruction of the Gog and Magog juggernaut (Ezek. 38-39), the rise of the antichrist, and the treaty with many signatories. Presumably the latter will permit the rebuilding of the temple.

2) Do you think God would approve of New Covenant Christians who are followers of Jesus to financially contribute to the building of the Third Temple and the acquisition of a red heifer for Israel to ritually slaughter?

Yes. In my mind, this is really the same question as does God approve of Christians helping forward the Zionist vision which sought and obtained the restoration of the nation of Israel? If supporting Israel in general is okay, then supporting this particular aspect of Israel is okay. I would also note that God is going to own the temple as "the temple of God" and "the holy place" during the seventieth week. This is clear in Revelation 11:1-2. The Lord is looking forward to restoring the people and nation of Israel as his people during the seventieth week, and offering them all their OT promises through faith in their Messiah. This means that he was deeply involved providentially with the restoration of Israel as a nation, that he is deeply involved right now with preserving Israel for his purposes, and that he is deeply involved with the temple and red heifer projects in the background, ensuring that everything will be in place when the church is removed and the Lord returns to the people and nation of

Israel. Now if God is interested in Israel, her defense, her temple, and her post-rapture status, then I think believers ought to show an interest in these things too. Israel may be the enemy of God because of the gospel, but she is beloved of God because of his election. Perhaps this yes should be qualified. Our primary giving to Israel should be focused on evangelism, showing them that they do not reject Judaism when they believe on the Messiah but rather become a fulfilled Jew.

3) Does God providentially provide for the rebuilding of the temple and the procurement of the ashes of the red heifer?

Yes. As mentioned in the above paragraphs, God is working behind the scenes to have all the pieces in place when he removes the church as his earthly testimony and returns to Israel as his earthly testimony. While still in the 69th week and ostensibly working with Israel as his people and with his disciples as a saved remnant, he was working to have all the pieces in place to bring the church into existence. When the time came to tear the veil at the cross, his disciples were ready for the inauguration of the church, which occurred at Pentecost. In a similar way, the pieces are being put together now during the church age for a return to Israel for the final week of the seventy weeks. During the earthly dispensation of the 69th week, the spiritual preparations for the church age went largely unnoticed. But during the heavenly dispensation of the church age, the preparations for the seventieth week and its earthly dispensation are almost impossible to miss, at least for those with discernment.

Pete Garcia (Rev310.net)

1) Should Christians be excited about all the preparations for the coming Third Temple and red heifer ritual slaughter?

I believe that Christians shouldn't be overly fixated on any single Third Temple activity, but rather, on the convergence of all these activities coming together in our day. As the old saying goes,

Israel is God's prophetic timepiece. If that is true (and I believe it is), then the nation of Israel is God's hour hand, Jerusalem is God's minute hand, and the temple mount is God's second hand. The fact we are seeing: Israelis increasingly turning their attention to the building of a Third Temple, while simultaneously, Saudi Arabia (and other major Islamic players) losing interest in the Temple Mount is a huge shift in the theological-geopolitical landscape. Furthermore, we are seeing the proposed train system gaining traction within Israel to connect the Ben Gurion airport in Tel Aviv, to the Temple Mount in Jerusalem, which is equally amazing. Now, five 'perfect' red heifers arriving in Israel, which we still have to wait and see, are simply signs upon signs that the 70th Week of Daniel is about to begin, which means, our redemption draws even closer.

2) Do you think God would approve of New Covenant Christians who are followers of Jesus to financially contribute to the building of the Third Temple and the acquisition of a red heifer for Israel to ritually slaughter?

I don't propose to know the mind of God on these matters, but I can't see how God approves of anything that directs people's attention (or focus of affection) away from His Son, Christ Jesus in this dispensation. However, God has used people in the past (ex. Lord Balfour, President Truman, President Nixon, President Trump, etc.) to continue moving the prophetic ball forward according to His timeline. I suppose it will all come down to whether or not these perhaps well-intentioned Christians were doing what God called them to do, or if they were trying to "help" bible prophecy along of their own accord.

3) Would God providentially (or miraculously) provide circumstances (politically, etc.) and materials for the rebuilding of the Third Temple and red heifer ritual slaughter without officially endorsing it?

No, because an omniscient God cannot do anything without His own consent. Nevertheless, according to numerous passages in the Bible (Dan. 9:27, Matt. 24:15, 2 Thess. 2:7-8, Rev. 11), we know a third Jewish temple is going to be rebuilt. Now, whether the Jews are rebuilding this because they think their messiah has arrived (for ex. Rav Shlomo Yehuda Beeri), or because of the arrival of the Two Witnesses, is anyone's guess here in the present. We just know it is going to be rebuilt, but we are not certain as to why they decided to do it. However, the prophetic conditions seem to indicate a 'clearing of the plate' so to speak on the Temple Mount with the events of Ezekiel 38-39. The potential destruction of its current tenants (i.e., the Dome of the Rock and the Al Aqsa Mosque) seems to make rebuilding the temple in their absence an irresistible situation that the Antichrist will one day desecrate, thus fulfilling the prophetic word.

Derek Gilbert (SkywatchTV and Gilbert House You Tube Channel)

1) Should Christians be excited about all the preparations for the coming Third Temple and red heifer ritual slaughter?

The excitement Christians should feel about the preparations for the Third Temple, including the recent revelation that several candidates for the red heifer required for the ritual purification of the kohanim who will serve in the Third Temple, is the anticipation of Christ's imminent return. These preparations are simply indicators that the time until His return is short.

2) Do you think God would approve of New Covenant Christians who are followers of Jesus to financially contribute to the building of the Third Temple and the acquisition of a red heifer for Israel to ritually slaughter?

I honestly hadn't given thought to this question before now. The Temple Institute certainly directs much of its marketing to well-meaning Christians in the West. We are told by friends in Israel that

American and Chinese Christians are a major source of income for the Institute.

I think it comes down to what is in one's heart. If contributions are made out of a love for Israel and the Jewish people, without a clear understanding that building the temple is not required for Christ's return, or that building the temple would lead to the reinstitution of the sacrifices described in the Law, then God will probably be forgiving. However, it's clear from scripture that we Christians should understand that Jesus' sacrifice was the one to end all sacrifices. We don't need to shed any more blood. And, though this may surprise many Christians, our friends who live in Israel tell us most Israelis don't want a Third Temple! They believe that system ended when the Romans destroyed Herod's temple in 70 AD. The synagogue is where religious Jews worship today, so a Temple is no longer needed—besides the fact that building the Third Temple on the Temple Mount would trigger a regional war, if not World War III.

In fact, some Israelis consider the Temple Institute a fundraising scheme to finance the political goals of the haredim (ultra-Orthodox Jews).

3) Would God providentially (or miraculously) provide circumstances (politically, etc.) and materials for the rebuilding of the Third Temple and red heifer ritual slaughter without officially endorsing it?

It's possible that conditions for building the Third Temple might suddenly appear. God may allow it, to borrow a phrase from my wife, as a test and a trap. It's my view that Jewish eschatology may lead some to welcome the wrong character as Mashiach, and anyone who facilitates the building of a new temple on Mount Moriah would be identified by many as that man.

Dr. JB Hixson (Notbyworks.org)

1) Should Christians be excited about all the preparations for the coming Third Temple and red heifer ritual slaughter?

Yes... I think most definitely. It is a sign of the times that could very well indicate the soon-coming of Christ.

2) Do you think God would approve of New Covenant Christians who are followers of Jesus to financially contribute to the building of the Third Temple and the acquisition of a red heifer for Israel to ritually slaughter?

I think there are two ways to look at this. Prophetically speaking, I do not think it has any bearing. We cannot hasten the return of the Lord. In terms of wisdom, does it make sense for Christians to be supporting rituals in unbelieving Israel? Probably not. But I do not see this as a moral issue. We love Israel and we know God has a future for national Israel. So as long as a believer feels he or she is helping to lay the groundwork for true Jewish worship in the future (i.e., during the first half of the Tribulation), there is probably no harm in it. But I personally would not do it because it does not seem wise to me to invest in unbelieving Israel.

3) Would God providentially (or miraculously) provide circumstances (politically, etc.) and materials for the rebuilding of the Third Temple and red heifer ritual slaughter without officially endorsing it?

Well, of course, God can "providentially" do anything. That's kind of the meaning of the term. Throughout history God has used pagan enterprises to accomplish His purposes. He used Israel's enemies, for example, to discipline His people. So, I see no problem with God orchestrating the rebuilding of the temple in unbelieving Israel without officially endorsing their worldview.

Tom Hughes ("Hope for our Times" broadcast)

1) Should Christians be excited about all the preparations for the coming Third Temple and the red heifer ritual slaughter?

I would say yes and no. The yes is because we know that there's going to be a temple that's going to be built and we understand the ceremonies are going to take place again. There's going to be sacrifices and offerings. We get that. So, when we look at it from that perspective, a temple being built, red heifers, it's exciting because it's a sign that Jesus is coming again.

However, the problem is we also look at it and realize the coming temple is something that the Antichrist is going to sit in. He's going to be there demanding to be worshiped as God. He's also going to turn his persecution towards the Jews at that time. So, it's a heartbreaking thing when at the same time I'm excited about Jesus coming back. However, I'm very concerned about the Jews, the nation of Israel, and the deception that is also involved in the coming temple.

2) Do you think God would approve of New Covenant Christians who are followers of Jesus to financially contribute to the building of the Third Temple and the acquisition of a red heifer for Israel to ritually slaughter?

I am not somebody that would engage in doing that. I had a friend I was talking with recently about that and he said, "Look at it like this." He said, "What if somebody said, 'Hey, I'm just contributing to supply the nails that are going to crucify Jesus on the cross?'" And when you think of it like that, I think that's a very good perspective of it because we understand the dynamics that are behind everything that's there.

So, I would not encourage people to engage in funding something like that, although I myself have done in the past. Since then, I don't do it anymore. I don't think it's a good use of my funds.

3) Would God providentially (or miraculously) provide circumstances (politically, etc.) and materials for the rebuilding of the Third Temple and red heifer ritual slaughter without officially endorsing it?

That's a that's a hard question. So, I guess we can go back to 1948 and say, okay, when we look at all the different prophecies regarding the second coming of Christ, Israel's going to be a nation again. In 1967, they're going to have Jerusalem again. You fast forward and we realize that still in the future there is a coming temple.

The sacrifices will begin again. Was God part of 1948, gathering them back together? Part of 1967? Yes. He gathered them. We know from Ezekiel Chapter 37, gathering in unbelief. It will eventually turn into that place of belief. We get that. But was God acting in 1948 and 1967? Yes. So, as we look at a coming temple, the red heifer's, we know it's similar.

God has laid out a plan and God is moving everything in that direction. Does He endorse it? Well, He must endorse it in the sense of His word, tells us what's going to come. So in that regard, yes. And we know all prophecy is going to be fulfilled, every part of it. Daniel 9. What happens with the 70 weeks? Well, part of the prophecy is the temple, and it is the sacrifices that will begin again. God says that He will fulfill every single one of His prophecies.

Dr. Nathan Jones (Christ in Prophecy - Lamb and Lion Ministries)

1) Should Christians be excited about all the preparations for the coming Third Temple and red heifer ritual slaughter?

Yes, Christians should be excited that the Third Temple has been so well planned and prepared for, as it points to its soon construction, which means the even sooner return of Jesus Christ. While the Bible doesn't say what conditions lead to the Jews finally being able to build the Temple on the Temple Mount in place of or adjacent to the Dome of the Rock, the most likely scenario is the stunning victory of God over Islam in the Gog-Magog War of Ezekiel 38-39. A secondary possibility is that the Antichrist's peace treaty enforces the Jewish claim to building on the Temple Mount. Either way, construction seems right around the corner, and so then does the Rapture and subsequent return of Jesus Christ to set up His Millennial Kingdom and true Temple.

2) Do you think God would approve of New Covenant Christians who are followers of Jesus to financially contribute to the building of the Third Temple and the acquisition of a red heifer for Israel to ritually slaughter?

Not at all. The Third Temple and its sacrifices have been nullified by Christ's New Covenant. To contribute to the Third Temple is to contribute to binding people to Judaism and the sacrificial system which does not save. Christians have far better ventures to invest their money into which would benefit people toward Christ and His salvation.

3) Would God providentially (or miraculously) provide circumstances (politically, etc.) and materials for the rebuilding of the Third Temple and red heifer ritual slaughter without officially endorsing it?

"For who has known the mind of the Lord?" (Romans 11:34a)

Tim Moore (Christ in Prophecy - Lamb and Lion Ministries)

1) Should Christians be excited about all the preparations for the coming Third Temple and red heifer ritual slaughter?

Christians should be excited about any fulfillment of Bible prophecy, because it demonstrates the validity of the Word of God, the power and providence of the Almighty, and the imminence of Jesus' return. I am convinced that the Third Temple will not actually be constructed before the Church is removed from the world at the Rapture and the Antichrist is revealed. He will sign a peace treaty with the Jewish people, allowing them to finally construct their temple in Jerusalem.

But, just as the appearance of Christmas decorations in the fall affirms that Christmas -and Thanksgiving! - is just around the corner, these signs foreshadow the coming of our great God and Savior, Jesus Christ. In addition, these signs prove once again that God has not washed His hands of the Jewish people. He still plans to bring a great remnant of them to salvation. The fact that Jews are still identifiable as a people group on the earth is yet another validation of the promise and providence of God.

2) Do you think God would approve of New Covenant Christians who are followers of Jesus to financially contribute to the building of the Third Temple and the acquisition of a red heifer for Israel to ritually slaughter?

I think God works in ways far beyond our comprehension, but that He inspires individual Christians to serve Him individually. So, there is no question that He will motivate some to support Jewish efforts to fulfill the prophecies outlined in Scripture. That was true a century ago when Christian Zionists avidly supported the Jewish effort to return to the Promised Land and reestablish a home and a nation. Christians do not believe Israel represents a separate means of salvation apart from our Jewish Messiah, but we take seriously God's admonition to bless His chosen people.

Likewise, we do not believe that the Third Temple will offer forgiveness of sins through a reconstituted sacrificial system - or that the red heifer in and of itself is significant. As Hebrews 10:4 recognizes, "it is impossible for the blood of bulls and goats to take away sins." But, we also know that God's prophetic Word will be fulfilled, and that in the end the Jews will look upon the perfect

Sacrifice and weep over Him like the bitter weeping over a firstborn (Zechariah 12:10).

3) Would God providentially (or miraculously) provide circumstances (politically, etc.) and materials for the rebuilding of the Third Temple and red heifer ritual slaughter without officially endorsing it?

Clearly, God works all things together for our good and His glory. Even the pitiful schemes of Satan are turned in ways we do not always understand. Perhaps we can gain perspective on the Third Temple if we consider the first two.

David was inspired to build God a temple to replace the tent where the Ark of the Covenant dwelled. Nathan initially affirmed that inclination, but then returned with a word from God. The LORD asked rhetorically, "did I speak a word with any of the judges of Israel, whom I commanded to shepherd My people Israel, saying, 'Why have you not built Me a house of cedar?'" (2 Samuel 7:7, repeated in 1 Chronicles 17:6) His clear insinuation was that He had not demanded a temple of wood and stone, but rather hearts that were fully devoted to Him.

Samuel established this same truth when he said, "Has the LORD as much delight in burnt sacrifices as in obeying the voice of the LORD? Behold, to obey is better than sacrifice, and to heed than the fat of rams" (1 Samuel 15:22).

Still, God did honor David's desire to build for Him a temple—although He did not allow David himself to build it. Solomon built the first temple. Later, He took offense when the exiles who returned from Babylon neglected the building of the Second Temple - not because He lacked for a dwelling, but because their attitude reflected hearts that were far from Him.

The Second Temple was eventually completed and later made larger and grander by the great builder, Herod. In terms of official endorsement, however, even Jesus did not heap praise on the structure of the temple itself or *endorse* Herod's work. Instead, He honored its intended purpose as a "house of prayer" (Matthew 21:13). Recalling the full text of Isaiah's prophecy Jesus cited, God promised that "even [foreigners] I will bring to My holy mountain and make them joyful in My house of prayer. Their burnt offerings and their sacrifices will be acceptable on My altar; for My house will be called a house of prayer for all the peoples" (Isaiah 56:7).

So, official endorsement or gracious acceptance? I think it depends entirely on the motive of the people doing the building and the sacrificing. If they seek to please and serve the LORD, then their inclination to worship God will be honored as David's was—and the Holy Spirit will draw them to believing faith in the Lord Jesus Christ. But if they think that a building or a bull will be sufficient to appease our holy God apart from the Gospel, then they are as deceived as those who cried out, "the temple of the LORD, the temple of the LORD, the temple of the LORD" in Jeremiah's day (Jeremiah 7:4).

In the end, we know that the Third Temple will be built, and that a red heifer will be sacrificed. In the fulness of time, those pre-seen historic events will give way to a time of Great Tribulation for the Jewish people. Only when they have come to the end of themselves will they cry out, Baruch Haba B'shem Adonai - "Blessed is He Who comes in the Name of the LORD!" Then Jesus Christ will return to earth in glory and power to ascend the mountain of the LORD and reign from the throne of David.

So, while I am fascinated by all the prophetic events that are swirling around us today and converging as never before, I am not fixated on any of them individually. Instead, I am watching and waiting—and listening for "a shout, with the voice of the archangel and with the trumpet of God", knowing that soon and very soon our Blessed Hope is coming for His Bride. Are you ready?

Dr. Larry Ollison (Larry Ollison Ministries)

1) Should Christians be excited about all the preparations for the coming Third Temple and red heifer ritual slaughter?

Third Temple Preparations:

A believer should be very excited about these current events. For one, it confirms that the word of God is true and what was prophesied is coming to past. Secondly, it clarifies that the interpretation of these prophecies are literal and not symbolic. Third, it's a sign that Jesus' return is closer than it has ever been.

Red Heifer Ritual:
Many Christians are uneducated about the Temple offerings and other offerings / rituals needed for the service and preparations.
   Fact:
   I.   The Church Age and the Temple existed side by side for 40 years.
   II. Followers of Jesus, and this includes the Disciples of Jesus, daily went into the Temple, even after the resurrection. They could not enter the Temple unless they were mikveh'ed (a ritual bath designed for the Jewish rite of purification). Why would they perform this, if they are all baptized in Jesus? Why would they have to be ritually purified if they are washed in the Blood of the Lamb? Yet, they still did it for years and it was not considered blasphemous for believers. Also, they are required to be sprinkled by the ashes of the red heifer to cleanse them in case they came across a dead body.

2) Do you think God would approve of New Covenant Christians who are followers of Jesus to financially contribute to the building of the Third Temple and the acquisition of a red heifer for Israel to ritually slaughter?

Christians financially contribute to the building of the Third Temple:
God knew they would be scattered and return back into the land. Rebuilding the Temple is part of their "Return" to God. It's a sign that God has shown them favor again.

"I will plant them in their land, And no longer shall they be pulled up From the land I have given them," Says the LORD your God. (Amos 9:15). The Jewish people know that the gentiles will help with this process. Even King Cyrus and Darius helped out with supplying resources for the Second Temple.

"Even those from afar shall come and build the Temple of the LORD. Then you shall know that the LORD of hosts has sent Me to you. And [this] shall come to pass if you diligently obey the voice of the LORD your God" (Zechariah 6:15).

Notice in Revelation, it's John who measures the Temple. It clearly states, it's the TEMPLE OF GOD!!! Not only the Temple of God is measured, but in total, three things are measured: 1) The Temple OF GOD; 2) The Altar; and 3) Those who worship there (The priest / Cohen / Sons of Aaron) and the Levis. "Then I was given a reed like a measuring rod. And the angel stood, saying, rise and measure the Temple of God, the altar, and those who worship there" (Revelation 11:1). Two of these three things physically exist today: the Altar and the Priests!

John writes and clearly states that this Third Temple is NOT the beasts/antichrist's Temple. It's God's and only God's Temple. A person can say it's theirs; Donald Trump could help build it and says it's his building. Even the antichrist can say it's his building. However, it does not matter which man or even any angel who decides to lay claim to this structure. It's God's House and He gives it to no one. Paul confirms this very point for the sign of the coming of the Lord: "Let no one deceive you by any means; for [that Day will not come] unless 1) the falling away comes first, and 2) the man of sin is revealed, the son of perdition, who opposes and exalts himself above all that is called God or that is worshiped, so that he sits as God in the Temple of God, showing himself that he is God" (2 Thessalonians 2:3-4).

Here we have two clear verses that this coming Third Temple is and always will be GOD's house. Just because the man of sin declares he's god in the Third Temple, does not make it the antichrist's Temple. IT WILL NEVER BE HIS HOUSE. For a believer to declare the next Temple as the antichrist's Temple is a direct, rebellious, and degrading of God's house, God's authority and God's complete sovereign ownership. Do we not understand that this is the sole purpose of the antichrist, to declare that God's possessions are his and that he is god?

Thus, now knowing, that John and Paul, under the direction of the Holy Spirit declared the Third Temple as God's Temple. Is it not a good thing that Christians contribute to the House of God? Especially if that very HOUSE resides in Israel, in Jerusalem on Mt, Zion. Would it be considered THE ABOMINATION, if it were not God's house? This proves the point that the great ABOMINATION THAT CAUSES DESOLATION, wouldn't be such a big deal, unless, it's done in God's land, in God's city, on God's Holy Mountain, IN GOD'S HOUSE. That is the ultimate sign of AN ABOMINATION.

Final point, in Jesus' days on this earth, before the resurrection, the state of the Israeli government, especially the Temple state, was at an all-time low. Corruption was rampant; High Priests serving in the Temple were not even sons of Aaron, but appointed by the highest bidder and influenced by the Roman government. Yet Jesus still called it, "My House!"

I. *And He said to them, "It is written, 'My house shall be called a house of prayer,' but you have made it a 'den of thieves'"* (Matthew 21:13).

II. *Then He taught, saying to them, "Is it not written, 'My house shall be called a house of prayer for all nations'? But you have made it a 'den of thieves'"* (Mark 11:17).

III. *saying to them, "It is written, 'My house is a house of prayer,' but you have made it a 'den of thieves.'"* (Luke 19:46).

Jesus confirms, 1) the complete corruption; 2) it's His house; and 3) more importantly, the entire purpose for the Temple is 'A HOUSE OF PRAYER!"

The Rabbi Maimonides agrees that most of the Second Temple era when Israel was controlled by the Greek or Romans, the Kohen Gadol's position was used for political power. Kohanim not from the line of Aaron (Levites) paid for the position to be the High Priest and used their power to favor the government instead of G-d. Once in a while, Sadducees would obtain the office and often Priests would die in the Holy of Holies because they were not worthy of being Kohanim Gedolim or because they corrupted the process of burning the incense." ~ (Rabbi Moshe Ben Maimon 1135 A.D. – 1204 A.D.)

Acquisition of the Red Heifer:
Revelation 11 confirms there will be a Third Temple, and in order for that Temple to operate, the ashes of the red heifer will have to be used. By confirming that this Temple and the other Temples are for a House of Prayer and its God's house, the red heifer is needed to cleanse the land, due to many years of bloodshed, cleanse the people who will enter it, and cleanse the articles needed for the service. The Book of Hebrews explains that it's the flesh that was needed of the ashes of the red heifer, and that Jesus has performed a higher cleansing that is on another level, to cleanse one's conscience (spiritually).

"For if the blood of bulls and goats and the ashes of a heifer, sprinkling the unclean, sanctifies for the purifying of the flesh, how much more shall the blood of Christ, who through the eternal Spirit offered Himself without spot to God, cleanse your conscience from dead works to serve the living God?" (Heb. 9:13-14).

3) Would God providentially (or miraculously) provide circumstances (politically, etc.) and materials for the rebuilding of the Third Temple and red heifer ritual slaughter without officially endorsing it?

I think the answers above help clarify the endorsements of these last day miracles. However, here are more proofs.
There have only been 9 red heifers since the time of Moses, until now. Jews look for the days of the tenth red heifer, as a sign of the coming of the Messiah. In 2022, now there are 5 perfect red heifers. Only God can create such an animal by nature and it is considered a modern-day miracle, and that God is restoring fellowship with His people once again.

Bill Salus (Prophecy Depot Ministries)

1) Should Christians be excited about all the preparations for the coming Third Temple and the red heifer ritual slaughter?

This is a bittersweet topic. On the sweet side, Christians can point out that the Third Temple was prophesied to become a reality in the end times. We find references to this in several passages such as Revelation 11:1-2, Matthew 24:15 and 2 Thessalonians 2:4. As such, the coming Third Temple can be used to eschatologically evangelize.

On the bitter side, this coming temple, although foreknown by God, is not endorsed by Him. The reinstatement of animal sacrifices by the Jewish people as part of the antiquated Mosaic Law, blatantly ignores the fact that Christ's sacrificial death upon the cross fulfilled the Law and ended the sacrificial system. Read Matthew 5:17-18, Romans 8:3-4 and Galatians 3:23-25.

2) Do you think God would approve of New Covenant Christians who are followers of Jesus to financially contribute to the building of the Third Temple and the acquisition of a red heifer for Israel to ritually slaughter?

I apologize if this next answer sounds facetious, but the Third Temple will be constructed with or without the financial contributions of Christians. So, why would a Christian waste their hard-earned funds on this project. There are far better ministries to tithe into. Especially, since the temple's intended activities of sacrifices and offerings are futile and not endorsed by God, Read Psalm 50:7-15.

According to Luke 22:19-20, Christ shed His blood in order to inaugurate a better New Covenant. Presently, atonement is available through Jesus Christ, and not the Red Heifer. Save your money and invest it wisely into the Kingdom of God.

3) Would God providentially (or miraculously) provide circumstances (politically, etc.) and materials for the rebuilding of the Third Temple and red heifer ritual slaughter without officially endorsing it?

One of the primary reasons the Jews want to build this temple and reinstate animal sacrifices is to hasten the coming of their Messiah. They reject Jesus Christ as the Messiah. Isaiah 28:14, appropriately accuses these Jewish leaders as *"scornful men, Who rule this people who are in Jerusalem."* As such, why would God go out of His way to help these Christ rejecting scornful rulers?

I don't see any reason that the LORD would providentially or politically sponsor this temple building effort. The reality that these scornful rulers are going to discover, is that the Third Temple doesn't hasten the First Coming of the Messiah, which happened about two thousand years ago, but it will hasten His Second Coming at the end of the Tribulation Period!

Dr. David Schnittger (Southwest Prophecy Ministries)

1) Should Christians be excited about all the preparations for the coming Third Temple and the red heifer ritual slaughter?

I believe Christians can be "excited" about the preparations for the Third Temple in that it does represent a fulfillment of Bible prophecy. This would be similar to our excitement at Israel becoming a nation in 1948 in fulfillment of Bible prophecy. I do not think the intention of the Temple Faithful is to build a Temple that will eventually be occupied by the son of perdition (2 Th 2:3, 4). It is not at all clear that this occupancy occurs with the willing participation of the Jews, as this occurs at the height of power by the antichrist (Rev 13). It is my understanding that the rebuilding of the Third Temple by the Temple Faithful, is in anticipation of the return of the Messiah. As Maurice Jaffe, president of the Jerusalem Great Synagogue said to me in April 1977, "it may be that the Messiah we anticipate and the One you worship are one and the same." We know that the spiritual blinders will be lifted for the Jewish remnant at the Second Coming (Zechariah 12:10).

2) Do you think God would approve of New Covenant Christians who are followers of Jesus to financially contribute to the building of the Third Temple and the acquisition of a red heifer for Israel to ritually slaughter?

I would relegate the answer to that to the category of "disputable things" dealt with in Romans 14:10-19. I default to Romans 14:19: "Let us therefore follow after the things which make for peace, and things wherewith one may edify another." I am fine with other Christians contributing to this project as long as they do not judge me for choosing *not* to contribute.

3) Would God providentially (or miraculously) provide circumstances (politically, etc.) and materials for the rebuilding of the Third Temple and red heifer ritual slaughter without officially endorsing it?

I believe that everything that occurs is by the providential will of God, but that does not answer your question. In regard to God's providence for this particular project, I believe the sovereign hand of God will GUARANTEE that every jot and tittle of His prophetic Word will be fulfilled to the letter. As to whether this constitutes the moral or "prescriptive" will of God, I have my doubts. After all Romans 10:25 states, "...blindness in part is happened to Israel, until the fulness of the Gentiles be come in." In my view, this reality should temper our view of, and participation in, projects by Jewish religious leaders.

It is for this reason that I think the term "Zionist Christian" should be used with qualification. In my personal view, I am reticent to add any adjectives to my status as a "Christian." I believe this term, if rightly understood, is all-encompassing.

By the way, the anticipation of the ashes of the Red Heifer go all the way back to the mid-1970s when I was just getting my start at Southwest Radio Church. All that to say that *patience* is required for the fulfillment of prophetic Scriptures.

Amir Tsarfati (Behold Israel)

Amir did not answer my questions specifically, but the following is from a public compilation from a Telegram post on Sept 17, 2022 and a YouTube post addressing this topic: https://www.youtube.com/watch?v=55lofyD8Zd4

"Allow me to be very honest with you and say that all things pertaining to the Third Temple in Jerusalem bring anything BUT excitement to me.

Whether it's the blueprints of the building that are ready, the training of people for animal sacrifice, or the periodical resurfacing of red heifers to the scene - They are but one more reason for us to pray for the salvation of Israel, not to rejoice with them.

The imagery of the red heifer is yet another foreshadowing of the sacrifice of Christ for believers' sins. The Lord Jesus was "without blemish," just as the red heifer was to be. As the heifer was sacrificed "outside the camp" (Numbers 19:3), Jesus was crucified outside of Jerusalem (Hebrews 13:11–12). And just as the ashes of the red heifer cleansed people from the contamination of death, so the sacrifice of Christ saves us from the penalty and corruption of death. To see the Jews rejoice in the shadow of the cow and reject the substance of Christ is sad.

Instead of us trying to guess how close the rapture is, why don't we all use these events to pray for the veil to be lifted and for the substance to be recognized. Israel is about to go through the biggest deception followed by a more terrible Holocaust than ever before. All of which is sadly connected to that temple as it will serve as the seat of a pseudo-messiah who will get his power, authority, and throne from Satan himself.

Therefore, we, who know the truth and are eagerly waiting for our savior to come and take us any day now, must refrain from celebrating these sad events of a blind nation that will suffer greatly. "But their minds were blinded. For until this day the same veil remains unlifted in the reading of the Old Testament, because the veil is taken away in Christ. But even to this day, when Moses is read, a veil lies on their heart. Nevertheless, when one turns to the Lord, the veil is taken away." (2 Corinthians 3:13-16).

The church should not be excited about the Third Temple, the church is not to be excited about those things that are actually going to deceive and confuse the Jewish people, to think they do have a way to God now, even without Christ. Yes, for the Jews it is a messianic sign. Yes, for the Jews, it is full of excitement. But for us, for us who know exactly what the Third Temple is going to bring about for the Jewish people... it is bad news. It is terrible."

Dr. Andy Woods

1) Should Christians be excited about all the preparations for the coming Third Temple and the red heifer ritual slaughter?

Should we be excited about those things? I would argue yes. Not because I'm trying to reverse the book of Hebrews and go back to animal sacrifice. That's not why I'm excited about it. I'm excited about it because those things have to be functioning for the tribulation period scenario to come into existence. And so, what I'm trying to say is, midway through the tribulation period, the Antichrist will go into the rebuilt Jewish temple and put an end to animal sacrifices.

That means by the time you get to the midpoint, there has to be a temple built and there has to be a sacrificial system implemented. So the fact that these things are starting to happen now, it shows me that the seven-year tribulation period is approaching, and the reason I'm excited about that is, I'm of the perspective that the rapture or the translation of the church takes place before the tribulation period even begins.

The signs of the tribulation period don't just tell me that the tribulation period is coming, but they tell me that the rapture is coming even faster. That's why I'm excited about it. It's like the old adage when you see the signs of Christmas, Santa Claus, Christmas tree lights, Christmas songs in the department store, you know that Thanksgiving is coming because Thanksgiving occurs earlier on the calendar than Christmas. So, yeah, that's why I'm excited about it.

2) Do you think God would approve of New Covenant Christians who are followers of Jesus to financially contribute to the building of the Third Temple and the acquisition of a red heifer for Israel to ritually slaughter?

I would say it's a freedom in Christ issue because I don't have a verse in the Bible that says, "thus saith the Lord, 'You shall never assist or contribute to that kind of a project.'" I mean, if a believer individually, through their own volition and conscience, feels called to be involved in that, I don't think there's any biblical prohibition against them.

However, I would say that being involved in that is not the primary purpose of the church. Jesus gave us our instructions in the Great Commission, and part of those is not to fund the red heifer and these kinds of things. So I'm of the view that God is pretty good at fulfilling his prophecies. Whether I help him or not, he really doesn't need my help. I don't see that as something I have to do. I don't see that as the primary calling and mission of the church collectively. But at the same time, if an individual Christian feels called to be involved in that, I don't see any prohibition against it. So, I would just look at it as kind of a freedom and Christ balance issue.

If you want to do that, I think you have the freedom to do it. Just don't put it on the whole church, universal or local, and say, you know, we all have to do this because that's not our primary mandate.

3) Would God providentially (or miraculously) provide circumstances (politically, etc.) and materials for the rebuilding

of the Third Temple and red heifer ritual slaughter without officially endorsing it?

I don't think God ever endorses animal sacrifices, at least the way we're describing it, because the book of Hebrews is very clear that Jesus is the fulfillment of the animal sacrifices. So when He fulfills his word, He's not doing it as an endorsement. This is what Israel in unbelief is going to do. These are the circumstances that are necessary for unbelieving Israel to one day become believing Israel.

That's how God is working. It's with the end goal of leading Israel to faith alone, in Christ alone. They've got to be knocked down before they look up. They've got to be in a situation where the Antichrist betrays them by putting an end to these things. And that's what's going to sort of shock them, if you will, into faith in the second half of the tribulation period. That's God's end product. That's his endgame. He can provide providentially for the rebuilding of these things for that purpose. But that shouldn't be misconstrued as God is applauding animal sacrifices in and of itself.

Chapter 9: Seeking a Balanced Biblical Outlook on the Red Heifer Movement

In the previous chapter, we had the opportunity to read the various opinions of prophecy teachers that God has raised up in these times. I love and respect these teachers and have interviewed almost all of them at one time or another. We know that each one of them love Jesus and His Word, and are operating according to the convictions that they have after years of studying the Scripture – but did you notice that not all of them agreed perfectly on the three questions that I asked? I actually think these variations are a positive element.

My goal in this chapter is to build a foundation for understanding the role of Israel in the plan of God, and how this plan will unfold in the final end of the age developments. I also want to address the current New Testament theological perspective of the Second Temple, and the secular and religious Jewish people today who do not have faith in Jesus as the Messiah. This foundational understanding will help by giving us a thoroughly Biblical framework for assessing the Third Temple developments, including the red heifer. I will tackle these topics first, and then give my opinion on the three questions which I asked my brothers.

What Does the New Testament Teach about the Second Temple and Its Destruction?

If you have not read chapter 7 of this book in a while, I encourage you to refresh yourself with the teaching there as it relates to Paul's heart for his unsaved Jewish brethren, and also the meaning of the red heifer as a type that pointed to the final sacrifice of Jesus. What we learn from the entire book of Hebrews and its history is that God's work through a temple (and sacrifices) was finished in this age at the time of Jesus. This whole topic can be very complicated, but we will try to take it one step at a time.

Jesus made a prediction to the woman at the well that there would soon come a time when people would worship the Father in spirit and in truth, which would not be connected to the city of Jerusalem (John 4:21-24). In addition, the Bible teaches us that when Jesus died, the veil of the Temple was torn in two from top to bottom. This provides a definitive miracle of God that He was starting something new that did not involve a physical temple (Matthew 27:51). We learn on several occasions that the institutions of the Second Temple were operating for a period of time after Jesus ascended into heaven, but that it's influence would slowly fade away into obsolescence. Paul writes concerning the Old Covenant, *"Indeed, in this case, what once had glory has come to have no glory at all, because of the glory that surpasses it. For if what was being brought to an end came with glory, much more will what is permanent have glory"* (2 Corinthians 3:10-11). Paul is contrasting the glory of the Old Covenant under Moses, versus the surpassing glory of the New Covenant under the Spirit. The Old Covenant glory was being brought to an end and replaced with the permanent glory of the New Covenant.

The author to the Hebrews writes something similar about the New Covenant versus the Old Covenant when he says, *"In speaking of a new covenant, He makes the first one obsolete. And what is becoming obsolete and growing old is ready to vanish away"* (Hebrews 8:13). At the time of the writing of that book, the Second Temple still stood, but the writer understood that it would soon be destroyed and that all the semblances of the Second Temple and the Old Covenant would be permanently removed and would vanish away. That happened in AD 70 and is a testimony to the fact that God was finished with the Second Temple and its sacrifices because Jesus fulfilled them.

It is important to note that the Second Temple was not evil, nor wicked, but was part of the revelation of God and was originally encouraged by God to be built (see Haggai 1:8). However, once Jesus came and fulfilled the Old Covenant system, it was replaced with the New Covenant and also a new high priesthood of Jesus through Melchizedek (Hebrews 7). In fact, we are told explicitly that this Old

Covenant Levitical system has now been annulled through the work of Jesus, and there is a change of the Law to the New Covenant system which in the present age does not require a physical temple. The author of Hebrews writes, *"Therefore, if perfection were through the Levitical priesthood (for under it the people received the law), what further need was there that another priest should rise according to the order of Melchizedek, and not be called according to the order of Aaron? <u>For the priesthood being changed, of necessity there is also a change of the law.</u> For He of whom these things are spoken belongs to another tribe, from which no man has officiated at the altar. For it is evident that our Lord arose from Judah, of which tribe Moses spoke nothing concerning priesthood. And it is yet far more evident if, in the likeness of Melchizedek, there arises another priest who has come, not according to the law of a fleshly commandment, but according to the power of an endless life. For He testifies: "You are a priest forever According to the order of Melchizedek." <u>For on the one hand there is an annulling of the former commandment</u> because of its weakness and unprofitableness, for the law made nothing perfect; on the other hand, there is the bringing in of a better hope, through which we draw near to God"* (Hebrews 7:11-19).

      Under the Old Covenant, sacrifices were required in order to demonstrate faith and obedience in following the commandments of God. Once the New Covenant was established at the last supper and finalized with the death and resurrection of Jesus, sacrifices were no longer required to please God (Luke 22:20). The veil was torn and access was granted to everyone, not through sacrifices, but through faith in Jesus. Hebrews 10:19-22 reads, *"Therefore, brothers, since we have confidence to enter the holy places by the blood of Jesus, <u>by the new and living way that he opened for us through the curtain, that is, through his flesh</u>, and since we have a great priest over the house of God, let us draw near with a true heart in full assurance of faith, with our hearts sprinkled clean from an evil conscience and our bodies washed with pure water."*

      The entire book of Hebrews was written primarily to Jews, declaring to them the insufficiency of the Levitical and Temple sacrifices. They served a holy purpose under the Old Covenant, but now that the New Covenant is established by the once and forever sacrifice of Jesus, any Jewish reliance on the Temple sacrifices would now be misplaced. He reminds them that those sacrifices NEVER could truly take away sins anyway, but were simply pointing to the final sacrifice that the Messiah Jesus accomplished. *"For since the law has but a <u>shadow of the good things</u> to come instead of the true form of these realities, it can never, by the same sacrifices that are continually offered every year, make perfect those who draw near... For it is <u>impossible</u> for the blood of bulls and goats to take away sins"* (Hebrews 10:1, 4).

    We know that the Second Temple was not destroyed until AD 70. This meant that there was a transition period between the New Covenant being established by the offering of Jesus, and the destruction and removal of the Second Temple decades later. We also must remember that the first believers in Jesus were Jews who had 1500 years of sacrificial history that God knew would be hard to break (see Acts 10:10-17 as one example). Therefore, it is no surprise that most of the Jewish believers in Jesus still maintained their traditions and visits to the Second Temple up until it was destroyed. We see Peter and John and the other apostles teaching in the temple precincts (Acts 2-5). Many years later we see Paul going to the Second Temple in order to make some offerings and seeking to evangelize in the courts (Acts 21). Did their visits to the then existing Second Temple mean that they did not believe the sacrifice of Jesus was not enough? Not at all.

    Peter stated quite clearly that the Law of Moses and all its commandments were a heavy yoke that none of them could handle. He also stated that the Gentiles would be saved by grace just like the Jewish believers under the New Covenant. He says: *"Now, therefore, why are you putting God to the test by placing a yoke on the neck of the disciples that neither our fathers nor we have been able to bear? But we believe that we will be <u>saved through the grace</u> of the Lord Jesus, just as they will"* (Acts 15:10-11).

What we learn is that God put His stamp of approval on the final sacrifice of Jesus by tearing the veil in the Holy of Holies. This act meant that any future sacrifices were no longer needed or demanded by God. Any sacrifice after this point would not be accepted as being legitimate. But, what about Paul and others participating in the Second Temple services? God did not command these sacrifices, but instead, I believe He allowed them in this transition period knowing that it would soon become irrelevant because the Second Temple would be destroyed just a few decades later. Understanding this transition period becomes important when assessing the current Third Temple rebuilding movement.

In addition, any offering of sacrifice that was done by the Jewish believers in this transition period were done by faith and in connection with their faith in Jesus. They most likely understood the theology of the book of Hebrews and that animals cannot provide any genuine forgiveness, but only the blood of Jesus. This becomes important when we discuss the idea of modern religious Jews building the Third Temple. Will God accept their sacrifices? The book of Hebrews would teach absolutely not. Why not? Because their offering of sacrifices is FAR different than what was taking place by the 1st century Jews. How so? Because those offerings by Paul and others were in tandem with faith in Jesus and His final offering. I think that God allowed them for a short period of time because they were offered through faith in the blood of Jesus. Those sacrifices still pointed to the once and for all sacrifice of Jesus.

Make no mistake. When the modern religious Jews begin to offer sacrifices in the coming Third Temple, they will NOT be mixed with faith in the once and for all sacrifice of Jesus. This is why I believe God will not honor their sacrifices. In fact, the non-messianic religious Jews today are not ignorant of the person of Jesus of Nazareth. Some of them are indifferent, but many of them despise and hate Jesus. This is one of the reasons that many of the ultra-orthodox Jews call Jesus "Yeshu." The name of Jesus in Hebrew is Yeshua, but they call Him Yeshu which also is an acrostic which means, "May His Name be Blotted Out Forever." This is blasphemy, but it is well known in many religious circles and sadly, this is the way that even secular people describe and call Jesus. I would hope that many of them are unaware of this acrostic association.

There is a piece of rabbinical tradition which I find surprising in that it is included in their Talmudic literature. Most NT scholars believe that Jesus was crucified around AD 30-33. There is some variation, but this is the general consensus. The Second Temple was destroyed in AD 70 which is approximately 40 years after Jesus ascended into heaven. The Talmud reads: "Forty years before the Temple was destroyed the chosen lot was not picked with the right hand, nor did the <u>crimson stripe</u> turn white, nor did the westernmost light burn; and the doors of the Temple's Holy Place swung open by themselves, until Rabbi Yochanon ben Zakkai spoke saying: 'O most Holy Place, why have you become disturbed? I know full well that your destiny will be destruction, for the prophet Zechariah ben Iddo has already spoken regarding you saying: 'Open thy doors, O Lebanon, that the fire may devour the cedars' (Zechariah 11:1).'" – Yoma 39b.

Interestingly, the crimson stripe was in reference to that which was tied to what we know as the scapegoat of the Day of Atonement (Leviticus 16:21-22). The crimson cloth is not mentioned specifically in the Biblical passage, but the rabbinical tradition holds that this red cloth was tied to the goat and that there also was another red cloth kept in the Temple precincts. When the goat was sent away and the sacrifices were completed, the red cloth would miraculously turn white as evidence that God forgave their sin and atonement was completed. Yet the above story in the rabbinical literature says clearly that this red cloth stopped turning white about 40 years before the Second Temple was destroyed. This is ancient evidence in their own writings that the sacrificial offerings of the Second Temple were no longer providing atonement for the Jews, and God showed this to them by not miraculously turning the red cloth to white as happened prior.

Is this story 100% true? I have no way to verify it, but I do find it to have a greater level of authenticity in that it is reported by the rabbis themselves with no explanation as to why. We understand the timing factor because it coincides exactly with the death and resurrection of Jesus as the final sacrifice and the implementation of the New Covenant. The Second Temple veil was torn and this miraculous event is found in the NT showing that God no longer required these Levitical sacrifices in order for anyone to have access to the Holy of Holies. This is powerful testimony which helps shape our understanding of how God will look at the coming Third Temple sacrifices.

As we conclude this section, we must remember what is at stake. God sent His beloved Son to die as a substitute for His people (Isaiah 53). Instead of responding with repentance and acceptance to the 3-year ministry of Jesus, they plotted to kill Him. A few days before Jesus was arrested, He told them this parable, *"Hear another parable. There was a master of a house who planted a vineyard and put a fence around it and dug a winepress in it and built a tower and leased it to tenants, and went into another country. When the season for fruit drew near, he sent his servants to the tenants to get his fruit. And the tenants took his servants and beat one, killed another, and stoned another. Again he sent other servants, more than the first. And they did the same to them. Finally he sent his son to them, saying, <u>'They will respect my son.'</u> But when the tenants saw the son, they said to themselves, 'This is the heir. Come, let us kill him and have his inheritance.' And they took him and threw him out of the vineyard and killed him. When therefore the owner of the vineyard comes, what will he do to those tenants?" They said to him, "<u>He will put those wretches to a miserable death and let out the vineyard to other tenants who will give him the fruits in their seasons.</u>" Jesus said to them, "Have you never read in the Scriptures: "'The stone that the builders rejected has become the cornerstone; this was the Lord's doing, and it is marvelous in our eyes'? Therefore, I tell you, the kingdom of God will be taken away from you and given to a people producing its fruits. And the one who falls on this stone will be broken to pieces; and when it falls on anyone, it will crush him." <u>When the chief priests and the Pharisees heard his parables, they perceived that he was speaking about them.</u> And although they* *were seeking to arrest him, they feared the crowds, because they held him to be a prophet"* (Matthew 21:33-46).

We learn several things from this parable. Jesus notes in the parable that the master of the vineyard (God) sent many servants (prophets) who were killed by the tenants (Jewish leadership). Finally, the master (God) believes that they will respect his son (Jesus). Instead, the tenants (Jewish leadership) kill the master's son. Jesus asks the Pharisees what they think the master will do in regard to the killing of the heir. They acknowledge that it would be correct to put the wretches to a miserable death and replace the leadership. Matthew writes that the chief priests and Pharisees knew this parable was speaking about them. Instead of repenting, they had thoughts of arresting Jesus.

About this same time, Jesus came into Jerusalem. *"And when He drew near and saw the city, He wept over it, saying, "Would that you, even you, had known on this day the things that make for peace! But now they are hidden from your eyes. For the days will come upon you, when your enemies will set up a barricade around you and surround you and hem you in on every side and tear you down to the ground, you and your children within you. And they will not leave one stone upon another in you, because you did not know the time of your visitation"* (Luke 19:41-44). Jesus pronounces a judgment on Jerusalem, the Temple, and its people because their leadership refused to recognize the time of His prophetic and long-awaited arrival. Because of their rejection, the city and the Temple would be destroyed, and many of its people would be killed in AD 70.

When God tore the veil in two from top to bottom, He provided miraculous evidence that the Old Covenant system of atonement through ceremonial sacrifice was over, and that any future such sacrifices would be rejected. Jesus was the final sacrifice. Even after the crucifixion, resurrection and ascension of Jesus, the people and their leadership refused to recognize their sin and continued to persecute His followers (Acts 3-12). Finally, after providing a 40-year window of witnessing to the people of Israel to accept His Son as the final sacrifice, God closed that window with the destruction of the Second Temple.

What is the Spiritual Condition of National Israel Today?

The title of this section is very carefully nuanced. I am talking about National Israel. Think of it as a corporate group like we find in the OT. Even when God sent National Israel into exile in the Babylonian captivity for their sin, there were faithful individuals like Daniel, Ezekiel, Jeremiah, and others who simply got caught up in the judgment of the entire nation. The leadership was wicked, and God most often judged the nation according to its leadership. We often don't understand this theological principle because today we are so individualized, but this was the way it was in the OT. Remember when David sinned by having a census in 2 Samuel 24? David was the one who sinned, but as a result of his sin, judgment came and 70,000 people died through a plague (1 Chronicles 21:14). David himself was not killed, but many of the people were. This is similar to when in the first century the Jewish leadership rejected Jesus and judgment came upon that entire generation (Matthew 11:16; 12:39, 41, 42, 45). Jerusalem and the Second Temple were destroyed, and hundreds of thousands were killed by the Romans.

Even during the destruction of Jerusalem, we know there were individuals who were saved, including some of the apostles, disciples, and others. It is the same today with National Israel. The Jewish leadership of Israel (including the religious Jews) does not embrace Jesus as Messiah, but there are individual Jews who are saved. So, as we discuss the following state of National Israel, let's remember that even though the people may be judged according to their nation, there are individuals who have become followers of Jesus the Messiah and are saved. It's also important to remember that even in the first century, Paul loved his Jewish brethren (Romans 9:1-5), but was still bold enough to call them lost and in need of salvation (Romans 10:1-5). This is still true today.

To further illustrate this thought, I receive questions from people all over the country every single day. Recently, I received the following question from a woman named Linda. She wrote, "I have some friends who go to a national denominational church. When I talk to them about prophecy and the nation of Israel, they say that the remaining promises to Israel were given to the church because of Israel's disobedience and murder of Jesus. They also point out that the modern nation of Israel is far from perfect. It is socialistic, secular, promotes LGBTQ, and is unfriendly to messianic Christians. They ask me how I can support such a godless nation that rejects Jesus and hinders Christian evangelism. What can I say?"

Here was my response:

There are two ways to respond to this question. One is theological and the other is prophetic. First, it is wise to simply acknowledge the truth of the assertions of your friends about the modern state of National Israel. It is well known that it was founded by secularist socialists who flirted with communism. If you study the history, many of the religious Jews were against the founding of the state of Israel because the founding fathers of modern Israel were so secular and atheistic. This was blasphemous to the religious Jews of the 19th and 20th centuries.

Second, we might ask the question, "In some ways how is this any different than the original founding of the nation in the book of Exodus?" Notice what God says to Israel through Moses as they were about to enter the promised land, "*Do not say in your heart, after the LORD your God has thrust them out before you, 'It is because of my righteousness that the LORD has brought me in to possess this land,' whereas it is because of the wickedness of these nations that the LORD is driving them out before you. <u>Not because of your righteousness or the uprightness of your heart</u> are you going in to possess their land, but because of the wickedness of these nations the LORD your God is driving them out from before you, and that <u>He may confirm the word that the LORD swore to your fathers, to Abraham, to Isaac, and to Jacob.</u>* "Know, therefore, that the LORD your God is not giving you this good land to possess <u>because of your righteousness, for you are a stubborn people.</u>*

Remember and do not forget how you provoked the LORD your God to wrath in the wilderness. From the day you came out of the land of Egypt until you came to this place, you have been rebellious against the LORD. Even at Horeb you provoked the LORD to wrath, and the LORD was so angry with you that he was ready to destroy you" (Deuteronomy 9:4-8).

Theologically, we learn that God did not give the land to Israel in ancient times because they were righteous, but to keep His promises to the patriarchs. Prophetically speaking, Israel today does not deserve the land any more than they did in ancient times. God did not bring back the people of Israel to the land in 1948 because they earned it (Ezekiel 36:24; 38:8). He brought them back into the land so He can fulfill His prophetic promises of the 70th week spoken of by Daniel (9:24-27), among other prophecies. He is going to judge them for their rebellion against His Son Jesus, purge and discipline them, but save the remnant as they call out on the name of Jesus at the end of the tribulation (Jeremiah 30:7; Hosea 5:15; Matthew 23:37-39; Zechariah 12:10; 13:8-9).

Why do we support the state of Israel today? We do not endorse everything they do. They are far from perfect as a government and a people. We support and love the state of Israel indirectly in a sense. Indirectly because we do not approve of them implicitly. More accurately, we support and endorse the Word of God, which contains promises to the nation of Israel that are still unfulfilled. Not a single time in Scripture are the promises to Israel ever transferred to the church. These promises will be fulfilled literally. Ultimately, we support and affirm the prophetic promises of God to and about Israel. God does not fully approve of Israel's actions today and neither should we, but God has not forsaken nor abandoned Israel (Jeremiah 31;35-37; Amos 9:8; Romans 11:25-29) and again, neither should we.

It is absolutely true what Jesus said that no one can be saved apart from faith in Him (John 14:6; Acts 4:12). It is pretty obvious that <u>secular</u> Jews anywhere in the world today are not saved. What about religious Jews who pray, read the Bible, and are waiting for the Messiah? Paul writes with great sorrow that <u>any</u> Jew who <u>does not</u>

<u>embrace Jesus is lost</u> and unsaved (Romans 10:1-3). Today, many religious Jews (especially in Israel) hate Jesus and Christians, sometimes aggressively.

That is how I answered Linda's question, but it fits perfectly into how we Christians who follow Jesus as the Messiah and final sacrifice should address the prophetic developments of the red heifer and building of the Third Temple.

I get asked often about those religious Jews who read and believe the Old Testament. They claim to pray to God the Father and also believe that His promises are true, but they reject Jesus as Messiah. We should always be friendly and loving and kind, and never are we ever to persecute or speak evil of anyone that does not embrace Jesus as Messiah. This is especially true of Jewish people because of church history which had much "Christian" persecution of Jews. This was wrong then and is wrong today.

At the same time, we need to interact with a few questions:
1) When Jewish people who reject Jesus as Messiah pray today, does God the Father hear their prayers?
2) Can a Jewish person have a relationship with God the Father if they reject Jesus?
3) Are the Jewish people who seem sincere in their desire to build a Third Temple pleasing God if they still try to please God apart from a faith in Jesus?
4) Is Judaism a genuine religion that God accepts?

These are all very good questions, and the New Testament speaks quite boldly on these issues. In fact, as we have seen, Jesus speaks clearly on this issue. He said to the apostles and to Israel in the first century, *"I am the way, the truth, and the life, no one comes to the Father, except through Me"* (John 14:6). Peter said, *"And there is salvation in no one else, for there is no other name under heaven given among men by which we must be saved"* (Acts 4:12). These are powerful and crystal-clear verses which answer the above questions. As difficult as it may be for some to accept, all of the answers to the 4 questions above are an unequivocal "NO."

A true and genuine religion is one that provides salvation, and any religion that does not embrace Jesus is false and cannot provide or secure salvation. I don't intend this to sound harsh, but it is true. Judaism, as a religion, does not nor cannot provide salvation because it rejects Jesus. Therefore, all the efforts by the religious Jews to fully reestablish Judaism and the Third Temple sacrifices are all fruitless efforts and do not honor the Son. Therefore, God cannot lie and accept their efforts when they reject His one and only Son whom He gave to die.

So, when a religious Jew prays, his prayers are not accepted by the Father unless they are prayed in the context of having a relationship with Jesus which they clearly do not. Jesus said, *"Whatever you ask in My name, this I will do, that the Father may be glorified in the Son"* (John 14:13; see also 15:16; 16:23, 24, 26).

Notice the consistent theme of the following verses:

John 5:23 *"That all may honor the Son, just as they honor the Father. Whoever does not honor the Son does not honor the Father who sent Him."*
John 15:23 *"Whoever hates Me hates My Father also."*
Luke 10:16 *"Whoever listens to you listens to Me, and whoever rejects you rejects Me, and whoever rejects Me rejects the one who sent Me."*
1 John 2:23 *"No one who denies the Son has the Father; everyone who confesses the Son has the Father also."*
John 5:45-46 *"Do not think that I will accuse you to the Father. There is one who accuses you: Moses, on whom you have set your hope. For if you believed Moses, you would believe Me; for he wrote of Me."*
1 John 2:21-23 *"I write to you, not because you do not know the truth, but because you know it, and because no lie is of the truth. Who is the liar but he who denies that Jesus is the Messiah? This is the antichrist, he who denies the Father and the Son. No one who denies the Son has the Father. Whoever confesses the Son has the Father also."*
John 15:18-21 *"If the world hates you, know that it has hated Me before it hated you. If you were of the world, the world would love you as its own; but because you are not of the world, but I chose you out of the world, therefore the world hates you. Remember the word that I said to*

you: 'A servant is not greater than his master.' If they persecuted Me, they will also persecute you. If they kept My word, they will also keep yours. But all these things they will do to you on account of My name, because they do not know Him who sent Me."

As you can observe from the above verses, these present a very stark and clear picture of the situation in the first century as well as today. It is impossible to honor the Father through prayer, Torah study, sacrifices, or building a Third Temple if it does not include honoring Jesus the Son. A person cannot know the Father without honoring Jesus as Messiah. In addition, if anyone rejects Jesus, they reject the Father who sent Jesus. If someone hates Jesus, they hate the Father. Even more bold, the above Scripture is saying that anyone who denies Jesus as the Messiah is a liar and is associated with the spirit of the antichrist. When the antichrist comes on the scene to deceive the Jews in making a covenant (Daniel 9:27), I believe that part of his covenant message will be to encourage the Jewish leadership to reaffirm a denial of Jesus as the Messiah.

When Paul was outlining the plan of God in seeking to reach the Gentiles, he writes, "*As far as the gospel is concerned, [the Jews] are enemies for your sake; but as far as election is concerned, they are loved on account of the patriarchs, for God's gifts and his call are irrevocable*" (Romans 11:28). This concept is important. Paul says that any Jewish person who rejects the gospel is an enemy in one sense, but God still loves them and has a plan for them in the future. We should love them also and pray for their eyes to be opened to God's only plan of salvation. This plan includes coming to faith in Jesus, but just because God loves them doesn't mean that God is going allow a separate way to come to Him. Jesus is the only WAY. If we have these truths in the back of our mind, we can begin to formulate some solid Biblical answers to the questions that were asked in the previous chapter.

My Answers to the Three Questions About the Red Heifer Movement

As we saw in the previous chapter, many of our favorite prophecy teachers shared their thoughts and wisdom on the discussion surrounding the red heifers and Third Temple. I deliberately did not read their comments fully before I wrote my own thoughts on the issue in this section. In this way, I am offering up my own thoughts with humility, and not with the idea of specifically contradicting or agreeing with any of the thoughts of my brothers knowingly. I am kind of excited to write my answers below and then go look to see how much we agree or maybe disagree. Either way, these are not salvation issues and so it is okay if we disagree on some of these minor points. I know all these brothers well, and we all understand the spiritual maturity of agreeing to disagree agreeably on non-salvation topics like this.

1) Should Christians be excited about all the preparations for the coming Third Temple and red heifer ritual slaughter?

I would absolutely say YES to this question, but we always have to frame our answers carefully. For whatever reasons, Christians have come to be quite opinionated on this issue. In the several interviews I have done on this topic, I have seen quite a varied response to these questions. Some people get very passionate and angry when someone answers in a way that they do not like. It is good to be a person of conviction, but the fruit of the Spirit is gentleness (Galatians 5:23). We are commanded to have an answer to defend the faith, but to do it in a spirit of gentleness and respect (1 Peter 3:15).

I have had the opportunity to write quite a bit lately on the Olivet Discourse and the book of Revelation concerning the 7-year tribulation. If you write down the characteristics of this time period as found in the Olivet Discourse and Revelation, it is quite scary. This is a time of unprecedented destruction upon the earth and the human race. The worst time in the history of the creation, including the flood, says Jesus in Mark 13:19. Jesus also said that if those days of judgment were not shortened to 7 years, the entire world of humanity would perish (Matthew 24:22). Am I excited about this? No, I am not.

We know that the preparations for the red heifer and the coming Third Temple are attempts by the religious Jews to seek after God apart from Jesus. They are trying to restore the Mosaic system of sacrifices which were ordained by God under the Old Covenant. They have rejected the sacrifice of Jesus and the institution of the New Covenant by Jesus which their own prophets foretold would be coming (Jeremiah 31:31-34; Ezekiel 37:26).

In addition, the religious Jews make an agreement with the antichrist, which begins the 70th week of Daniel (Daniel 9:27). They receive him as the messiah (John 5:43) and are deceived into reinstituting the sacrificial system and the finalization of the Third Temple. This is going backwards! Instead, they should be receiving Jesus, who is greater than Moses (Hebrews 3-4). These actions cannot please God as we saw above. Yes, they are embracing the Mosaic covenant, but it is a covenant that Jesus superseded. Therefore, this action of embracing the Old Covenant and denying the sufficiency of the sacrifice of Jesus is blasphemous. This will not and cannot be honoring to God because it does not honor the Son Jesus as we read in the verses above.

So, I am not excited about these events per se, but what I am excited about is that all the preparations are signs that Jesus is coming soon. He is coming first to rapture away His saints and receive them to Himself as He promised. Jesus said He is going away to the Father's house (in heaven) to prepare a place for us so that He will come back and receive us to Himself that we may go where He is going (John 14:1-3)! Now that is a great and precious promise, and so when we see the red heifer and Third Temple preparations happening, this reveals to me that the rapture is coming very soon! That gets me excited!

2) Do you think God would approve of New Covenant Christians who are followers of Jesus to financially contribute to the building of the Third Temple and the acquisition of a red heifer for Israel to ritually slaughter?

As a pastor and teacher for 25 years, I have been asked almost every Biblical question you could ever imagine. My response was always to ask for a verse. What does the Bible say? Another way to ask or answer this question is to frame it as, "is it a sin?" If I say that something is a sin, then I need to have a Bible verse to back me up. There is no specific verse in the Bible that prohibits a Christian from giving financially to the red heifer or Third Temple movement. What this means is that this answer comes down to being a Romans 14 issue. Romans 14 discusses those topics in which there is room for disagreement. In other words, this is not a salvation issue. We are to hold our opinions with love and respect towards our brothers or sisters that might disagree with us. We are not to judge them (Romans 14:3, 4, 10, 14).

Paul discusses issues that are not specifically written in the Bible. He says, *"All things are lawful for me– but not everything is beneficial. All things are lawful for me– but I will not be controlled by anything"* (1 Corinthians 6:12). He also writes something similar, *"All things are lawful, but not all things are helpful. All things are lawful, but not all things build up"* (1 Corinthians 10:23). We learn several principles from these two passages. The Bible does not give answers to every last question, so Paul says in one sense all things are lawful for him. He obviously does not mean that murder or adultery or stealing are lawful. He is saying that if the Bible does not address it specifically, it is okay for him to do, but he has some guidelines that he personally uses. 1) Not everything is beneficial; 2) He will not do things that lead to addiction (controlled); and 3) Not everything edifies or builds up others or himself.

Each person has to come to their own conviction in answering this second question. What would I do personally? I could not in good conscience donate financially to the red heifer movement nor to the

Third Temple movement. Why? The main reason is that I would rather see my money go to ministries or missionary efforts that are proclaiming the gospel or teaching the New Covenant truths which are things that clearly communicate the only way of salvation. That is my conviction, but I am not going to judge anyone else for their decisions. That is between them and the Lord as Romans 14:10 tells me.

At the same time, I would like to address two other items which I have seen coming on the horizon. There are some Christians who are advocating and supporting the Third Temple with a sincere desire for unity. They desire to see peace and harmony between Jews, Christians, and Muslims on the Temple Mount. Shouldn't we all desire to see peace and harmony? Of course, but we must ask at what cost? Jesus said, *"And He was teaching them and saying to them, "Is it not written, 'My house shall be called a house of prayer for all the nations'? But you have made it a den of robbers"* (Mark 11:17; quote of Isaiah 56:7).

I have heard some Christians say that one of the motives of those desiring to build the Third Temple is to make this a house of prayer for all nations and fulfill Scripture. I think this is taking the passage in Isaiah 56:7 and Mark 11:17 out of context. Originally, in the time of Isaiah, the Jews were supposed to be a light to the surrounding nations. Solomon also thought of the 1st Temple as a house that could draw foreigners to worship the one true God (1 Kings 8:41-43). Sadly, Israel did not fulfill this vision and when we come to the time of Jesus, God started a new age of gospel evangelization that did not involve a specific location (John 4:21-24). This means that any attempt to try and reestablish an Old Covenant Temple system is an affront to the New Covenant works that Jesus brought to be through His death and resurrection. The veil of the Second Temple was torn from top to bottom as we read earlier. The physical temple system era is over until Jesus builds a new temple in the millennium (Ezekiel 40-48). Presently, the new and living way into the holy of holies is found through a relationship with Jesus and not a physical temple (Hebrews 10:19-21). Again, seeking to have unity through a physical temple administered by Jews under the Old Covenant is going backwards, especially for a Christian who should understand thoroughly the theology as found in the New Testament and specifically the book of Hebrews.

Additionally, I am not sure how prayer would actually work in the Third Temple. Certainly, the Jews would set up a holy of holies, an outer court, a woman's court, a court of the gentiles far outside the inner precincts. They might invite a Gentile Christian to come pray in that outer court, but will they allow them to pray overtly in the name of Yeshua (Jesus)? This is highly doubtful. Why would a Christian be content praying in an outer court when we know that veil to the holy of holies was torn in two by God and we have access to the real holy of holies? It seems contradictory and misleading. We would be pacifying our Jewish friends instead of letting them know in love that their efforts are not going to bring about salvation.

Can a Christian join together with a Jewish person or a Muslim and pray together in unity? This is impossible, as we know that we would be committing blasphemy in implying that we all worship the same God. The Muslim denies that Allah has a son, and we know if you do not honor the Son, you do not honor the Father. This is also true with Judaism. They would clearly say that the God they worship does not have a son either, and they certainly reject Jesus. Jesus said that if they reject Him, they automatically are rejecting the Father whom they claim to worship. We cannot have it both ways.

One last comment. There are those I have seen comment that say since Paul provided offerings in the Second Temple (Acts 21), this justifies a Christian today offering something in a future Third Temple. This is apples and oranges. The Second Temple veil was torn miraculously and God allowed a transition period of 40 years, after which He destroyed that Temple as a testimony of judgment against the Jewish leadership for murdering His Son. That Second Temple was built under the authority and commandment of God by the prophets, and Jesus came and honored it with His presence. It had God-given authority, which slowly faded away until God removed it.

These actions today of building a Third Temple were never commanded by an authoritative prophet of God and are done in accordance with an overt rejection of the final sacrifice of Jesus. In fact, it is overt rebellion against Jesus and His message. It is apostasy. This is serious and quite different than what we find in the full context of Acts 21.

3) Would God providentially (or miraculously) provide circumstances (politically, etc.) and materials for the rebuilding of the Third Temple and red heifer ritual slaughter without officially endorsing it?

I can answer this with an absolute YES. When we look at Biblical history, we know that God has a grand plan that He seeks to accomplish. A few examples show this to be true. The first can be seen in the life of Abraham. God blessed Abraham with Sarah and her servant, Hagar. God did not cause Abraham to sin with Hagar, but he did this without consulting God. Even though He provided Hagar in His sovereign kindness to Sarah, God did not endorse Abraham's actions with Hagar. God also providentially allowed the Ishmaelites to arrive at the exact time that Joseph was in the pit. They took him to Egypt and God raised him up to be 2nd highest position in Egypt. God did not cause the brothers to do this, but they took advantage of the situation and sold him into slavery. Joseph says in Genesis 50:20 that what they meant for evil, God meant for good. God gave the Israelites gold and silver as they left and plundered Egypt (Exodus 3:22; 12:36). Yet they had a choice and used this same gold, which a gift from God, and used it for evil in making the golden calf (Exodus 32).

If we look at modern history, there are many stories of miracles that took place during the 1948 war of independence, as well as the 1967 Six-Day war. Does this mean that God endorses all of modern Israel's behavior because He continues to protect them? It does not. It means that God has a greater purpose in mind and that is the salvation of Israel. He miraculously brought them back to the land

and continues to rescue them from all their enemies surrounding them to this day.

This is because God is working His sovereign plan out in order to bring them into the tribulation period, so that He can discipline and bring them to faith and salvation through His Son Jesus, whom they will look upon and weep (Zechariah 12:10).

In the same way, I see the red heifers and other opportunities that are being providentially given in order to accomplish His greater plan of salvation. They are still responsible, and they should repent of these efforts and receive Jesus as Savior and Messiah.

Chapter 10: Concluding Thoughts on the Red Heifer Movement

Where do we go from here? My goal was to provide the reader with a definitive book that gives a Biblical framework to understand the various prophetic developments that are happening in connection with the red heifers and the Third Temple. Even though there have been various red heifers appearing through the years, we currently have five potential candidates in the land of Israel that are expected to be ready for slaughter as early as November 2023.

Even if the current five red heifers should somehow become disqualified, the religious Jews have made tremendous progress to prepare for the construction of a Third Temple and will not give up their efforts to find a qualified red heifer to slaughter in their ritual. I am hoping that if the day of the red heifer slaughter comes and passes that this book will still provide an understanding of what has occurred and a solid Biblical Christian response to the event.

After almost 2,000 years, we certainly seem to be on the cusp of Bible prophecy to see the purifying of the Temple Mount and the construction of a Third Temple, thereby setting the stage for the events of the 7-year tribulation. We are living in exciting times, but at the same time they are heartbreaking times. Jesus wept over Jerusalem as He predicted its destruction due to the Jewish rejection of Him (Luke 19:41-44; 21:21-24; 23:37-41).

Just as Jesus wept over the situation in the 1st century, we should have a somber attitude at what is coming for our Jewish friends who have not yet received Jesus as Messiah during the coming 70th week of Daniel. It is called the time of Jacob's trouble and it certainly will be a time of great distress (Jeremiah 30:7; Mark 13:19).

So how should we prepare now? Most important, we need to be continually equipped to answer and evangelize those around us as to the prophetic signs that are happening in the present time. We know that God wants us to always be ready to give a defense for the hope that we have (1 Peter 3:15). As the world gets worse and worse (2 Timothy 3:13), we can take hope and comfort that Jesus has already won the war and we look forward to the return of Jesus to get His bride.

During these times of prophetic fulfillment, let us not forget that we are all sinners (Romans 3:23) and none of us are perfect (Romans 3:10). The payment for our sin is death. We all deserve it (Romans 6:23). That is the bad news. But isn't it great that God gives us good news. God shows His love to us in that, while we were still sinners, Jesus died in our place (Romans 5:8). If we repent of our sins and ask Him to forgive and save us, we can be confident that we will escape the coming 7-year tribulation as well as eternal judgment (Romans 10:9; 1 Thessalonians 1:10; 5:9; Romans 5:9). I encourage you to make sure you have sought the Lord and are ready for His return.

May the Lord bless you as you seek Him. I encourage you to check out Prophecy Watchers (prophecywatchers.com) and our podcast at TheWeekInBibleProphecy.com where we will continue to keep you informed and updated on the prophetic times in which we live.

Jesus said: *"And what I say to you, I say to all: Watch!"* (Mark 13:37).

Appendix 1: Alfred Edersheim and The Temple, Its Ministry and Services as They Were at the Time of Jesus Christ

Alfred Edersheim was a Jew who became a Messianic believer and who studied the rabbinical writings along with the Old Testament. He wrote extensively on the NT from a Jewish perspective. I recommend his writings as a good background to understand the Jewish frame of reference. He died in 1889.

This section below is from *The Temple, Its Ministry and Services as They Were at the Time of Jesus Christ.* (London: James Clarke & Co., 1959), 351–355.

Significance of the Red Heifer

This is not the place more fully to vindicate the views here propounded. Without some deeper symbolical meaning attaching to them, the peculiarities of the sin-offering of the red heifer would indeed be well-nigh unintelligible.[1] This must be substantially the purport of a Jewish tradition to the effect that King Solomon, who knew the meaning of all God's ordinances, was unable to understand that of the red heifer. A 'Haggadah' maintains that the wisest of men had in Eccl. 7:23 thus described his experience in this respect: 'All this have I proved by wisdom,' that is, all other matters; 'I said, I will be wise,' that is, in reference to the meaning of the red heifer; 'but it was far from me.' But if Jewish traditionalism was thus conscious of its spiritual ignorance in regard to this type, it was none the less zealous in prescribing, with even more than usual precision, its ceremonial.

---

[1] It is impossible here fully to explain our views. All the more we bespeak for them a calm and candid examination. Christian writers in this country, whether theological or popular, have either passed over the subject, or (like Fairbairn, *Typology*, vol. 2. p. 376) taken too superficial a view to require special notice.

The first object was to obtain a proper 'red heifer' for the sacrifice. The *Mishnah*[2] states the needful age of such a *red heifer* as from two to four, and even five years; the color of its hide, two white or black hairs springing from the *same follicle* disqualifying it; and how, if she have been put to any use, though only a cloth had been laid on her, she would no longer answer the requirement that upon her 'never came yoke.'

The Sacrifice of the Red Heifer

Even more particular are the Rabbis to secure that the sacrifice be properly offered.[3] Seven days before, the priest destined for the service was separated and kept in the Temple—in 'the House of Stoves'—where he was daily sprinkled with the ashes—as the Rabbis fable—of all the red heifers ever offered. When bringing the sacrifice, he was to wear his white priestly raiments. According to their tradition, there was an arched roadway leading from the east gate of the Temple out upon the Mount of Olives—double arched, that is, arched also over the supporting pillars, for fear of any possible pollution through the ground upwards. Over this the procession passed. On the Mount of Olives the elders of Israel were already in waiting. First, the priest immersed his whole body, then he approached the pile of cedar-, pine-, and fig-wood which was heaped like a pyramid, but having an opening in the middle, looking towards the west. Into this the red heifer was thrust, and bound, with its head towards the south and its face looking to the west, the priest standing east of the sacrifice, his face, of course, also turned westwards. Slaying the sacrifice with his right hand, he caught up the blood in his left. Seven times he dipped his finger in it, sprinkling it towards the Most Holy Place, which he was supposed to have in full view over the Porch of Solomon or through the eastern gate. Then, immediately descending, he kindled the fire. As soon as the flames burst forth, the priest, standing outside the pit in which the pile was built up, took

---

[2] *Parah*, 1. 2.
[3] *Parah*, 3. 4.

cedarwood, hyssop, and 'scarlet' wool, asking three times as he held up each: 'Is this cedarwood? Is this hyssop? Is this scarlet?' so as to call to the memory of every one the Divine ordinance. Then tying them together with the scarlet wool, he threw the bundle upon the burning heifer. The burnt remains were beaten into ashes by sticks or stone mallets and passed through coarse sieves; then divided into three parts—one of which was kept in the Temple-terrace (the *Chel*), the other on the Mount of Olives, and the third distributed among the priesthood throughout the land.

Children used in the Offering

The next care was to find one to whom no suspicion of possible defilement could attach, who might administer purification to such as needed it. For this purpose a priest was not required; but any one—even a child—was fit for the service. In point of fact, according to Jewish tradition, children were exclusively employed in this ministry. If we are to believe the *Mishnah*,[1] there were at Jerusalem certain dwellings built upon rocks, that were hollowed beneath, so as to render impossible pollution from unknown graves beneath. Here the children destined for this ministry were to be born, and here they were reared and kept till fit for their service. Peculiar precautions were adopted in leading them out to their work. The child was to ride on a bullock, and to mount and descend it by boards. He was first to proceed to the Pool of *Siloam*,[2] and to fill a stone cup with its water, and thence to ride to the Temple Mount, which, with all its courts, was also supposed to be free from possible pollutions by being hollowed beneath. Dismounting, he would approach the 'Beautiful Gate,' where the vessel with the ashes of the red heifer was kept.

Next a goat would be brought out, and a rope, with a stick attached to it, tied between its horns. The stick was put into the vessel with the ashes, the goat driven backwards, and of the ashes thereby

---

[1] *Parah*, 3. 2–5.
[2] Or *Gihon*. According to Jewish tradition, the kings were always anointed at Siloam (1 Kings 1:33, 38).

spilt the child would take for use in the sacred service so much as to be visible upon the water. It is only fair to add, that one of the Mishnaic sages, deprecating a statement which might be turned into ridicule by the Sadducees, declares that any clean person might take with his hand from the vessel so much of the ashes as was required for the service. The purification was made by sprinkling with hyssop. According to the Rabbis,[1] three separate stalks, each with a blossom on it, were tied together, and the tip of these blossoms dipped into the water of separation, the hyssop itself being grasped while sprinkling the unclean. The same authorities make the most incredible assertion that altogether, from the time of Moses to the final destruction of the Temple, only seven, or else nine, such red heifers had been offered: the first by Moses, the second by Ezra, and the other five, or else seven, between the time of Ezra and that of the taking of Jerusalem by the Romans. We only add that the cost of this sacrifice, which was always great, since a pure red heifer was very rare,[2] was defrayed from the Temple treasury, as being offered for the whole people.[3] Those who lived in the country would, for purification from defilement by the dead, come up to Jerusalem seven days before the great festivals, and, as part of the ashes were distributed among the priesthood, there could never be any difficulty in purifying houses or vessels.

---

[1] *Parah*, 11. 9

[2] It might be purchased even from non-Israelites, and the Talmud relates a curious story, showing at the same time the reward of filial piety, and the *fabulous* amount which it is *supposed* such a red heifer might fetch.

[3] Philo erroneously states that the high-priest was sprinkled with it each time before ministering at the altar. The truth is, he was only so sprinkled in preparation for the Day of Atonement, *in case* he might have been unwittingly defiled. Is the Romish use of 'holy water' derived from Jewish purifications, or from the Greek heathen practice of sprinkling on entering a temple?

Appendix 2: Josephus Discusses the Red Heifer

Josephus was a 1st century Jewish historian who participated in the great revolt against Rome in AD 66-70. He was a Jewish general in the Galilee who was captured and became a historian primarily for Rome.

6. (78) Then it was that Miriam, the sister of Moses, came to her end, having completed her fortieth year[c] since she left Egypt, on the first day[d] of the lunar month Xanthicus. They then made a public funeral for her, at a great expense. She was buried upon a certain mountain, which they call Sin; and when they had mourned for her thirty days, Moses purified the people after this manner: (79) He brought a heifer that had never been used to the plough or to husbandry, that was complete in all its parts, and entirely of a red color, at a little distance from the camp, into a place perfectly clean. This heifer was slain by the high priest, and her blood sprinkled with his finger seven times before the tabernacle of God; (80) after this, the entire heifer was burnt in that state, together with its skin and entrails; and they threw cedar wood, and hyssop, and scarlet wool, into the midst of the fire; then a clean man gathered all her ashes together, and laid them in a place perfectly clean. (81) When therefore any persons were defiled by a dead body, they put a little of these ashes into spring water, with hyssop, and, dipping part of these ashes in it, they sprinkled them with it, both on the third day, and on the

---

[c] Josephus here uses this phrase "when the fortieth year was completed," for when it was begun; as does St. Luke, "when the day of Pentecost was completed," Acts 2:1.

[d] Whether Miriam died, as Josephus's Greek copies imply, on the first day of the month, may be doubted, because the Latin copies say it was on the tenth, and so say the Jewish calendars also, as Dr. Bernard assures us. It is said her sepulcher is still extant near Petra, the old capital city of Arabia Petraea, at this day; as also that of Aaron, not far off.

seventh, and after that they were clean. This he enjoined them to do also when the tribes should come into their own land. [7]

---

[7] Flavius Josephus and William Whiston, *The Works of Josephus: Complete and Unabridged* (Peabody: Hendrickson, 1987), 107.

Made in the USA
Middletown, DE
03 September 2023